The Good Woman of Setzuan

BERTOLT BRECHT

The Good Woman of Setzuan

English Version by Eric Bentley

University of Minnesota Press
Minneapolis

Published by the University of Minnesota Press
111 Third Avenue South, Suite 290
Minneapolis, MN 55401-2520
http://www.upress.umn.edu

Printed in the United States of America on acid-free paper

Library of Congress Cataloging-in-Publication Data

Brecht, Bertolt, 1898–1956.
    [Gute Mensch von Sezuan. English]
    The good woman of Setzuan / Bertolt Brecht ; English version by
Eric Bentley.
       p.   cm.
    Originally published in *Parables For the Theatre: Two Plays by
Bertolt Brecht* (Minneapolis: University of Minnesota Press, 1948).
    Includes bibliographical references.
    ISBN 0-8166-3527-7 (alk. paper)
    I. Bentley, Eric, 1916–   II. Title.
PT2603.R397G813   1999
832'.912 — dc21   99-045732

The University of Minnesota is an equal-opportunity educator and employer.

10 09 08 07 06 05 04 03   10 9 8 7 6 5 4 3

Contents

Preface   vii
  Eric Bentley

Comments on *The Good Woman of Setzuan*
from *Bentley on Brecht*   xi
  Eric Bentley

The Good Woman of Setzuan   1

Selected Bibliography   109

Preface

Eric Bentley

I have completed three distinct English versions of *The Good Woman of Setzuan*. The first (a collaboration with Maja Apelman) was published by the University of Minnesota Press in 1948 as half of the volume *Parables for the Theatre*. The second I made on my own for Uta Hagen and the Phoenix Theatre, New York, in 1956. The third (a collaboration with Michael Rice) I made in the 1980s and revised it for production by the Pulse Theatre, New York, in 1998. For this last occasion the title was shortened to just *The Good Woman* and may be further shortened later to *goodwoman* (yes, one word, lowercase).

Which of the three should be reprinted now in 1999? Version 1 is literal and complete, and if it included a few errata, they could easily be corrected. Version 3 is up-to-date in the 1990s and could also be called up-to-place given that, largely through Michael Rice's music, it has become an American work that could take its place beside Hal Prince's Broadway shows. But we are sticking with version 2 here because it has worked well on stage, indeed on a number of stages, and has found avid readers, worldwide, in editions by Grove Press and Penguin Books.

This second version does not contain every word of the German. Sometimes, with some plays, I well knew, it would be good to reproduce every word of the original German. I met this standard (well, almost) with my version of *The Caucasian Chalk Circle* (now being reissued by Minnesota along with the present volume). *Good Woman* was a different case. Even in the German it is somewhat diffuse, and even in Frankfurt I had watched intelligent audiences dozing off. Along with Ms. Hagen, whose first language is German, I decided the English version would benefit by cutting. Not just a word here and there—anything that is diffuse in German will be much more diffuse when translated into English. Whole passages must be cut, we decided, even a short scene or two. If you don't believe me, or if you have scholarly instincts and wish to check up on me, go to the library and read the first Minnesota edition, from which nothing had been cut.

Some scholarly readers, over the years, have been upset by the title *The Good Woman of Setzuan*. The nearest Chinese restaurant offers Szechwan (or perhaps Sechuan) cooking. What is this word Setzuan? It is a transcription from Brecht's Sezuan. Szechwan and Sechuan signify a Chinese province, and Brecht or his editors must have found that out, if rather late in the game. But Sezuan in the manuscript Bertolt Brecht gave me to translate was a town. In the English, I have held on to the form Setzuan.

Woman? The German says *Mensch,* which means a human being of either sex, and feminists now want the word "Person" to replace the two words "human being," so I get letters asking why the play is not called *The Good Person of,* well maybe *Sechuan,* maybe *Szechwan,* maybe... The word "Person" had stuck in my throat because traditionally it has so often carried, as dictionaries acknowledge, a suggestion of belittlement ("nice little person"). So why not change the title for the English version?

This human being is a woman. Is that a weak word, a *soft* word, as one critic of my title has said? Depends if you think all women are weak and soft. Brecht was consulted about the changed title and agreed to it.

Two bits of version 3 could profitably be used in productions of version 2 or any other version: the addition of a foreword and a revision of the old epilogue, now called an afterword.

Foreword
Threepenny Opera you have seen
And heard old Peachum say
"The world is poor, and men are bad"
Which still is true today.

But Peachum is not God, whereas
In the play you'll now be seeing
We'll put three gods, all rather good,
And one good human being.

A legend with a heart of gold
Has just occurred to us:
A fairy tale we shall unfold
Exotic . . . fabulous . . .

A human being, who is good
Her prayers to heaven sending!
Surely the gods must listen and
Provide the happy ending?

Afterword
That's hopeless. Hope-less. Stop if you don't mind!
No hope — for our play — or for mankind!
We *hoped* you all would see today
A happy ending for Shen Te.
(Unhappy endings were expected too

For bad guys like Ms. Shin and Mr. Foo.)
Ladies and gentlemen, don't be angry, please!

A golden legend floated on the breeze
A fairy tale, exotic... fabulous...
And now, what's been slipped up on us?
We're stuck. We don't know what to do
So... may we... pass the buck... to you?
YOU show us, YOU demonstrate, my friends,
How a good woman might reach good ends.
Show us what's what and which is which:
HOW CAN WE MORTALS BE BOTH GOOD AND RICH?
YOU write the happy ending to the play:
There must... there must... there's got to be... a way.

Comments on
The Good Woman of Setzuan
from *Bentley on Brecht*

Eric Bentley

The text of this section is taken from notes on *Good Woman* that I wrote for a Christian Gauss Seminar at Princeton in 1960. It subsequently became part of an introduction to *Seven Plays by Bertolt Brecht* and of an essay in *The Brecht Commentaries* and *Bentley on Brecht*.

Anna-Anna. Already in *The Seven Deadly Sins,* Brecht had made of his usual antithesis — kind *vs.* cruel, humane *vs.* inhumane, natural *vs.* unnatural, idealistic *vs.* realistic — a division within the same person. The world being bad, the good person requires a bad "half" if he is to survive. In this proposition, there is no contradiction between Brecht's natural constitution and Marxism, provided the negative side be identified with capitalism. Even the key role of the economic motive was something Brecht had worked out on his own: in *A Man's a Man,* written before the conversion to Marxism, we find Uriah only able to hold on to Galy Gay by the lure of a "deal."

Drama schematic and abstract. Brecht did not like the word *abstract.* He made a personal motto of the phrase "truth is concrete." And in this, most of the literary world, on both sides of the Iron Curtain, agrees with him. But what are they all agreeing to? The word *concrete* is an abstraction, and all art is abstracted from life, with considerable subtraction and distortion along the way—just think of the Brecht menagerie!

But I would not try to empty the antithesis concrete/abstract of all meaning. It makes sense to say *The Three Sisters* presents life more concretely than does the *Oresteia*; and it is a fact that writers today emulate this concreteness rather than that abstractness. Even so, most nonmodern drama was more abstract, and modern drama continually reverts to relative abstractness. After Ibsen (concrete), Expressionism (abstract).

Brecht believed that he reinstated the concrete. But did he? On the contrary, beginning with *A Man's a Man,* he created a dramaturgy as schematic and abstract as any workable dramaturgy well could be. With its numbering, its blackboard demonstrations, its many unashamedly two-dimensional characters, it is surely the abstractest thing in drama since the Spanish *autos* of the seventeenth century. Nor am I speaking merely of the *Lehrstücke*. Beginning with *A Man's a Man,* and not least in *The Good Woman of Setzuan,* Brecht's drama is all schematic and abstract—more so perhaps than is acceptable to the larger theater public of many countries today.

A Man's a Man has the form of a scientific demonstration. One draft actually ends with the words "Quod erat demonstrandum." *The Good Woman* is similar. As in the earlier play, the first sequence of action presents a premise or hypothesis. Then comes the action, which is divided into clearly demarcated sections, each proving its own point. As Shen Te puts it at the end, she had only tried:

1. to help her neighbor
2. to love her lover
3. to keep her little son from want.

These are the three main sections and "actions" of the play. When Shen Te has failed in all three respects, even with increased help each time from her alter ego Shui Ta, she makes her appeal to the gods. There is nothing they can do. Q.E.D.

It sounds dismal! And what could have been a worse fate for the theater than the theories and "schemes" of Brecht without his talent, which so often works, not hand in hand with the theories and "schemes," but at daggers drawn with them? This much must be conceded to those who abhor the schematic and the abstract: the schematic and the abstract never amount to theater, drama, literature, art *by themselves.* Yet, if what is added is not the "concrete" characterization and milieu that we are used to, what is it? In other words:

What is Epic Theater, actually? In the first instance, a misnomer. And this Brecht, in effect, has admitted. The word *epic* suggests too many things or the wrong things. In England and America, there is the added trouble that our schools don't make much use of the old triple division of literature: epic, lyric, dramatic. There is a lot to be said for *not* using it, as the dramatic is not a separate genre running parallel to the others without touching them. The dramatic has traditionally embraced epic and lyric elements.

But "epic" does make a good antithesis to "lyric." In *Illusion and Reality,* Christopher Caudwell makes them so different it would be hard to conceive of the same person excelling at both, harder still to find him combining the two in one work. Caudwell's theory, oversimplified, is that the lyric writer writes himself while the epic writer writes the world. Even my oversimplification helps in explaining Brecht, who was originally a "lyric" poet, but who, when he discovered the world, tried to do without the self altogether and create a wholly "epic" drama.

Brecht never really succeeded in writing a novel — i.e., never became a fully epic writer. He remained the Poet as Playwright, and if we speak not of intentions but attainments, we should call his theater a lyric theater. The name would certainly bring out his qualities, rather than his defects.

There are defects — or perhaps deficiencies would be the word — in the area where the novelist or epic writer excels, namely, in the full presentation of individual character. Brecht would show at his worst in a comparison with Ibsen. But Ibsen — the "modern" Ibsen, that is — would show at his worst in a comparison with Brecht: for he has cut out the lyric element by the roots.

Lyric theater would also prove a misleading term. There would be confusion with opera — or with decorative drama written in verse like, say, Christopher Fry's plays. Caudwell's formula guides us to a deeper interpretation of the lyric: the writer's relation to all of life is always at stake in it. The "lyricism" of *The Good Woman of Setzuan* is not isolated in the songs or bits of spoken verse. Rather, these are emanations of the spirit in which the whole play is composed. The prose, too, is poetry — not decorative, but of the essence.

Epic theater is lyric theater. The twentieth century has seen a series of attempts to reinstate poetry in the theater. Brecht made the most successful of these attempts. How? If it was not because he was a better poet — and one can scarcely maintain that he was a better poet than Yeats or Eliot — why was it? Cocteau's phrase "poetry of the theater" as distinct from "poetry *in* the theater" helps us toward the answer. As early as 1920, Eliot had completely debunked the kind of drama that is poetic chiefly in consisting of mellifluous or even exquisite lines. Nonetheless, his own interest continued to be in the poetic line and the way it was written: the free verse of *The Cocktail Party* is offered as an alternative to the blank verse and stanzas of the Victorians. Now, though Brecht too had his alternative forms of dialogue to offer, they are but a part of a Grand Design to replace the Victorian drama in all departments. And it is the design as a whole that provides the answer to the question: what kind of lyric theater? The poetry *of* the theater is not a poetry of dialogue alone, but of stage design, of lighting, of acting, and of directing. Nor is it enough that these be "imaginative" — to use Robert Edmond Jones' word for his vision of a poetry of the theater —

they must also be called to order — subordinated to the statement which is being made. For this theater is no fireworks display. It is not there to show off the theater arts, together or individually, but to show off the world around us and the world within us — to make a statement about that world. Hence, while Jones' designs often look better in a book than on the stage, photographs of the Brechtian stage, thrilling as they are, fall short of doing justice to the phenomenon itself. There is this difference too. Jones was adding his own vision to that of an author: two inevitably somewhat disparate contributions were made toward what would be at best a happy combination. In the Brecht theater, though others made contributions, he himself laid the foundation in every department: he was the stage designer, the composer, and the director. The production as a whole, not just the words, was the poem. It was in essence, and often in detail, *his* poem.

Collaboration. It has not escaped attention that, following the title page of a Brecht play, there is a page headed: *Mitarbeiter* — Collaborators. It has only escaped attention that these names are in small type and do not appear on the title page of the book or, presumably, on the publisher's royalty statements.

All the collaborators, and many who have witnessed the work of collaboration, have testified to Brecht's penchant for collaborating. We learn that at one period he didn't like to write alone and seated but only pacing the floor and talking with several "collaborators." We hear of his willingness to snap up a phrase or notion supplied by an onlooker.

Yet Brecht had no talent at all for collaboration if the word carries any connotation of equality, of give and take. His talent was for domination and exploitation, though the ethics of the procedure were in this sense satisfactory, that his collaborators were always people who wanted and needed to be dominated and exploited. That this should be true of friends and mistresses who never wrote anything notable of their own goes without saying. It is true also of the Big Names, including the biggest name of all—that of Kurt Weill. Weill has no more enthusiastic and enthralled listener than myself: the glory of his music for *Mahagonny* and the other Brecht works is not in question. But how was that success achieved? Brecht sometimes intimated that he himself contributed some or all of the tunes of *The Threepenny Opera.* For years I considered this a boast. Later I came to believe it. For I saw the way Brecht worked with composers, and I listened to the music Weill wrote before and after his collaboration with Brecht. Weill took on the artistic personality of any writer he happened to work with. He had no (artistic) personality of his own. For a theatrical composer this is conceivably an advantage. I am not arguing that point. I would only mention in passing that what is true of Weill, is true of Eisler. The music of both is parasitic. When parasitic upon Brecht, it is nearly always superb. Parasitic upon second-raters, it is second-rate. And when they attempt music that is not parasitic at all, music that is bolstered by no writer, music that is not imitative of any composer, or even music that is not in some sense serious or flippant, a parody of other music, they court disaster.

What kind of stage designs has Caspar Neher made for other playwrights? Often, very good ones, but in what way? Either in his Brecht style or in some established mode that would not mark off his work from that of any other eminent modernist. The "originality" of Neher is concentrated in the work he did for Brecht. Since that work was inspired *by* Brecht, it is clear that the word originality is in need of redefinition.

Brecht dominated not only the collaborators who were present in the flesh but also the dead or absent writers whose works he adapted. *The Threepenny Opera* is not a "steal" but a new work and just as "original" as John Gay's *Beggar's Opera.* In no case can the success or the character of a Brecht work be attributed to the writer or writers whom he drew upon. Though you might, for example, believe that Brecht "ruined" *The Pri-*

vate Tutor, by that very token you can hardly attribute the proven effectiveness of the new play to Lenz.

What is interesting is not the legal issue of plagiarism — a hare started by Alfred Kerr long ago — but a critical problem: how was it that Brecht arrived at his results in this particular way? Perhaps the burden of proof is on those who regard the opposite procedure as normal, since it is only in recent times that "life" and not literature has come to be regarded as the usual source for a dramatist's plots and characters. The most "original" playwright of all, Shakespeare, is also the one who keeps scholars busiest studying his literary sources. Molière said he took his material wherever he found it — and the place he meant was literature or the theater, not "life." Why did Brecht return to the earlier method? The question can hardly be answered *en passant,* but one thing is clear: that in exploring the whole range of dramatic art Brecht rediscovered the many-sided significance of collaboration.

The heart of the matter is that the individual artist contributes less to his art than is commonly supposed. A large contribution is always made by collaborators, visible and invisible. Drama, being narrative in a concentrated form, relies even more on the collaboration of others than does fiction. The dramatist draws on more "conventions" as a welcome shortcut — conventions being unwritten agreements with the audience. He is inclined to use, not the raw material of life, but material that has already been "worked" by another artist. It takes all sorts of collaboration to make dramatic art, the final collaborative act being that which unites performer and spectator.

The book from which most comments on this last subject are — directly or indirectly — taken is *The Crowd* by Gustave LeBon. There is a fatal equivocation in it. LeBon fails to distinguish between the crowd in the concrete (say, 1000 people of any kind in a theater) and the crowd in the abstract (the proletariat, the masses, etc.). Slurring over this simple difference, he enjoys himself reaching unwarranted conclusions.

In English we would call the first phenomenon the audience, and the second the public; and it occurs to me that English is unusual in having these two words. In French the audience is called *le public,* in German, *das Publikum.* Language seems to put English-speaking persons in immediate possession of a useful distinction.

We have heard much, too much, of the contribution the audience makes to a show. The audience laughs or cries, is attentive or fidgety, creates an atmosphere, sets up a current of psychic electricity between itself and the players.... All of which is to speak of the problems that arise at the end of the whole process of writing and rehearsing. No essential problem can be solved at that late point, as has a hundred times been shown in the history of American out-of-town try-outs, without anyone's learning the lesson.

The audience's collaboration is one thing, the public's is another. There comes to mind Synge's historic statement that all art is a collaboration between the artist and his people. Synge correctly observed that something had gone terribly wrong in modern times. In my terms: the problem of the modern theater is the problem, not of the audience only, but of the public.

One sign of this is that your audience problem can often be solved, while the problem of the public remains where it was. The problem of the audience has been that it has lacked homogeneity, common purpose, warmth. You can get these things by picking an audience of people united in a common faith. I would say T. S. Eliot solved the audience problem when he put on *Murder in the Cathedral* in the cathedral at Canterbury. Here is a theatrical "experiment" that succeeded. But that audience did not help Mr. Eliot to write his play. The public was not only not collaborating, it was absent, indifferent, even hostile.

Bertolt Brecht's radical reconsideration of theater and drama includes a reconsideration of both audience and public. The trade unions and other large groups who would buy out the house once a week in the Germany of the twenties obviously represented a new audience and might also suggest the idea of a new public that corresponds to a new working-class culture. Seen in this connection, Brecht's communism will not appear as unplausible as it does to many of his readers in America today. Such readers would do well to remember that an artist will accept almost anything if it seems to offer a future for his art.[1] Brecht accepted communism as Pascal advised accepting supernatural religion: as a bet according to which you have everything to gain and very little to lose. Concerned for the integrity of the theater art, Brecht looked to proletarianism as the only way in which the artist could regain the kind of collaboration which Synge in 1900 thought was barely available anymore.

Now, in his estimates of power and political success, Brecht showed shrewdness. At a time when the Soviet Union was considered weak, and the huge social-democratic movement in Western Europe tended to be anticommunist, Brecht put his money on Moscow. There is little need, in 1960, to explain what a sound investment that was — if political success is the criterion. What if we apply other criteria — especially the very simple one of an audience and a public for Brecht?

As far as the public goes, one normally considers it as collaborating with the artist while he is planning and writing. Brecht, however, believed that he belonged with the public of the future. Only socialism could give his works a home. He once told me in so many words that if world socialism did not come about he did not expect his works to have any future at all.

The Soviet Union gave Brecht the Stalin Peace Prize. East Germany gave him a place to live and a large subsidy for a theater. Does this amount to a public? Did Brecht's plays find their proper habitat? Did Epic Theater establish itself as the theater of the communist countries?

There was a small production of *Threepenny Opera* in Russia some thirty years ago! Despite the visit of the Berlin Ensemble in 1957, the Russians are still (1960) not doing any Brecht plays. Nor are most of the East German theaters. The failure to find a public is total. On the other hand, Brecht has found an enthusiastic audience. But it consists of just the sort of people he ostensibly didn't want — chiefly the intelligentsia of "decadent" Paris and London.

As for what Brecht really wanted, we find the same ambivalence in this field as in others. When in America, he was brave about being ignored on Broadway. "Why expect them to pay for their own liquidation?" he once said to me. But he fretted about it too, and made a few stabs at crass commercial success. His attitude to the avant-garde theater was similar. The "so-called avant-garde" was not important, but, "under certain conditions," it would take up his plays. "What conditions?" I once asked him. "Well," he replied, "if I were a Frenchman — or if I became the rage in Paris." And to be the rage in Paris — "intellectual," "advanced," almost "revolutionary" Paris — is, as far as worldly success goes, the highest achievement of Brecht to date.

Even aside from politics, it is questionable whether Brecht could have had what he wanted. There comes to mind Georg Lukács' statement that, in the great ages, the drama flowed "naturally" from the existing theater, while, from Goethe on, the poetdramatist rejects the theater, writes plays which are "too good for it," and then calls for the creation of the kind of theater which will be good enough for the plays. Brecht saw the weakness of the postGoethe position — without being able to escape it. If there is any theater you cannot see a man's plays naturally flowing from it is a theater that doesn't yet exist! If there is any public that is not a collaborator it is a public that isn't yet there! We all applaud the work of the Berlin Ensemble, but that institution is not the product of a new proletarian society. Its audience is the bourgeois avant-garde. Its leaders — Herr Engel and Frau Weigel — are noble relics of the culture of the despised Weimar Republic. As for Bertolt Brecht, the point is not so much that he didn't succeed in getting any plays written about the doings in East Germany, as that, if he had, they would inescapably have been the product of the mind and sensibility that made *In the Swamp*. East German literary critics have been happier with Thomas Mann, who made no bones about being bourgeois, than with this uncomfortable Bavarian rogue.

Has "The Good Woman of Setzuan" dated? This query is not as easy as it sounds, because all plays "date" in many respects, even though some go on being played and read forever. In this case, the question is, does the play belong irretrievably to the Depression era? It does presuppose general unemployment on the one hand, and, on the other, slave-driver capitalists, like those of the factory system in the classic era of capitalism as described by Marx and Engels. An audience which does not presuppose these things will not cry "How true!" as often as the author would like. Today's audience knows, for example, that the composer who in the thirties predicted the swift demise of American capitalism in *The Cradle Will Rock* is today writing another revolutionary opera with the help of money from Henry Ford.

But such changes in background are negative factors: they only explain why a play will not receive an artificial "lift" from the audience. To the extent that *The Good Woman* is a good play and not absolutely confined in relevance to the Depression, it can command an audience. I see no reason, for that matter, to try to limit the interpretation of Brecht's plays to what is known to be his own understanding of them. As Shaw would put it, he was only the author. He was neither the audience nor the arbiter. During the Stalinist era, *The Good Woman* presented a good picture of current tendencies in Soviet society, with Shui Ta as the necessary "realistic" correction of the earlier idealism, and Yang Sun as eventually a high Party functionary, rising by the path of Stakhanovism. More permanently, the two sides of Shen Te, as they arise from the divided nature of Brecht, express such a division for all of us — and the tendency thereto which exists *in* all of us.

NOTE

1. "Only by crawling on his belly can an unpopular and trouble-some man get a job that leaves him enough free time." Thus spoke (Brecht's) Galileo.

The Good Woman of Setzuan

Characters

WONG, *a water seller*

THREE GODS

SHEN TE, *a prostitute, later a shopkeeper*

MRS. SHIN, *former owner of Shen Te's shop*

A FAMILY OF EIGHT *(husband, wife, brother, sister-in-law, grandfather, nephew, niece, boy)*

AN UNEMPLOYED MAN

A CARPENTER

MRS. MI TZU, *Shen Te's landlady*

YANG SUN, *an unemployed pilot, later a factory manager*

AN OLD WHORE

A POLICEMAN

AN OLD MAN

AN OLD WOMAN, *his wife*

MR. SHU FU, *a barber*

MRS. YANG, *mother of Yang Sun*

GENTLEMEN, VOICES, CHILDREN *(three), etc.*

Prologue

At the gates of the half-Westernized city of Setzuan. Evening.
WONG *the water seller introduces himself to the audience.*

WONG: I sell water here in the city of Setzuan. It isn't easy.
When water is scarce, I have long distances to go in search of
it, and when it is plentiful, I have no income. But in our part
of the world there is nothing unusual about poverty. Many
people think only the gods can save the situation. And I hear
from a cattle merchant — who travels a lot — that some of the
highest gods are on their way here at this very moment. Informed sources have it that heaven is quite disturbed at all the
complaining. I've been coming out here to the city gates for
three days now to bid these gods welcome. I want to be the
first to greet them. What about those fellows over there? No,
no, they *work*. And that one there has ink on his fingers, he's
no god, he must be a clerk from the cement factory. *Those* two
are another story. They look as though they'd like to beat you.
But gods don't need to beat you, do they? (THREE GODS
appear.) What about those three? Old-fashioned clothes —

dust on their feet — they *must* be gods! *(He throws himself at their feet.)* Do with me what you will, illustrious ones!

FIRST GOD *(with an ear trumpet)*: Ah! *(He is pleased.)* So we were expected?

WONG *(giving them water)*: Oh, yes. And I *knew* you'd come.

FIRST GOD: We need somewhere to stay the night. You know of a place?

WONG: The whole town is at your service, illustrious ones! What sort of a place would you like?

The GODS *eye each other.*

FIRST GOD: Just try the first house you come to, my son.

WONG: That would be Mr. Fo's place.

FIRST GOD: Mr. Fo.

WONG: One moment! *(He knocks at the first house.)*

VOICE FROM MR. FO'S: No!

WONG *returns a little nervously.*

WONG: It's too bad. Mr. Fo isn't in. And his servants don't dare do a thing without his consent. He'll have a fit when he finds out who they turned away, won't he?

FIRST GOD *(smiling)*: He will, won't he?

WONG: One moment! The next house is Mr. Cheng's. Won't he be thrilled!

FIRST GOD: Mr. Cheng.

WONG *knocks.*

VOICE FROM MR. CHENG'S: Keep your gods. We have our own troubles!

WONG *(back with the* GODS*)*: Mr. Cheng is very sorry, but he has a houseful of relations. I think some of them are a bad lot, and naturally, he wouldn't like you to see them.

THIRD GOD: Are we so terrible?

WONG: Well, only with bad people, of course. Everyone knows the province of Kwan is always having floods.

SECOND GOD: Really? How's that?

WONG: Why, because they're so irreligious.

SECOND GOD: Rubbish. It's because they neglected the dam.

FIRST GOD (*to* SECOND): Sh! (*To* WONG) You're still in hopes, are you, my son?

WONG: Certainly. All Setzuan is competing for the honor! What happened up to now is pure coincidence. I'll be back. (*He walks away, but then stands undecided.*)

SECOND GOD: What did I tell you?

THIRD GOD: It *could* be pure coincidence.

SECOND GOD: The same coincidence in Shun, Kwan, and Setzuan? People just aren't religious anymore, let's face the fact. Our mission has failed!

FIRST GOD: Oh come, we might run into a good person any minute.

THIRD GOD: How did the resolution read? (*Unrolling a scroll and reading from it*) "The world can stay as it is if enough people are found (*at the word "found" he unrolls it a little more*) living lives worthy of human beings." Good people, that is. Well, what about this water seller himself? *He's* good, or I'm very much mistaken.

SECOND GOD: You're very much mistaken. When he gave us a drink, I had the impression there was something odd about the cup. Well, look! (*He shows the cup to the* FIRST GOD.)

FIRST GOD: A false bottom!

SECOND GOD: The man is a swindler.

FIRST GOD: Very well, count *him* out. That's one man among millions. And as a matter of fact, we only need one on *our* side. These atheists are saying, "The world must be changed because no one can *be* good and *stay* good." No one, eh? I say: let us find one—just one—and we have those fellows where we want them!

THIRD GOD (*to* WONG): Water seller, is it so hard to find a place to stay?

WONG: Nothing could be easier. It's just me. I don't go about it right.

THIRD GOD: Really?

He returns to the others. A GENTLEMAN *passes by.*

WONG: Oh dear, they're catching on. (*He accosts the* GENTLE-MAN.) Excuse the intrusion, dear sir, but three gods have just turned up. Three of the very highest. They need a place for the night. Seize this rare opportunity — to have real gods as your guests!

GENTLEMAN (*laughing*): A new way of finding free rooms for a gang of crooks. (*Exit* GENTLEMAN.)

WONG (*shouting at him*): Godless rascal! Have you no religion, gentlemen of Setzuan? (*Pause.*) Patience, illustrious ones! (*Pause.*) There's only one person left. Shen Te, the prosti-tute. She *can't* say no. (*Calls up to a window*) Shen Te!

SHEN TE *opens the shutters and looks out.*

WONG: Shen Te, it's Wong. *They're* here, and nobody wants them. Will you take them?

SHEN TE: Oh, no, Wong, I'm expecting a gentleman.

WONG: Can't you forget about him for tonight?

SHEN TE: The rent has to be paid by tomorrow or I'll be out on the street.

WONG: This is no time for calculation, Shen Te.

SHEN TE: Stomachs rumble even on the Emperor's birthday, Wong.

WONG: Setzuan is one big dung hill!

SHEN TE: Oh, very well! I'll hide till my gentleman has come and gone. Then I'll take them. (*She disappears.*)

WONG: They mustn't see her gentleman or they'll know what she is.

FIRST GOD (*who hasn't heard any of this*): I think it's hopeless. *They approach* WONG.

WONG (*jumping, as he finds them behind him*): A room has been found, illustrious ones! (*He wipes sweat off his brow.*)

SECOND GOD: Oh, good.

THIRD GOD: Let's see it.

WONG (*nervously*): Just a minute. It has to be tidied up a bit.

THIRD GOD: Then we'll sit down here and wait.

WONG *(still more nervous)*: No, no! *(Holding himself back)* Too much traffic, you know.

THIRD GOD *(with a smile)*: Of course. If you *want* us to move. *They retire a little. They sit on a doorstep.* WONG *sits on the ground.*

WONG *(after a deep breath)*: You'll be staying with a single girl — the finest human being in Setzuan!

THIRD GOD: That's nice.

WONG *(to the audience)*: They gave me such a look when I picked up my cup just now.

THIRD GOD: You're worn out, Wong.

WONG: A little, maybe.

FIRST GOD: Do people here have a hard time of it?

WONG: The good ones do.

FIRST GOD: What about yourself?

WONG: You mean I'm not good. That's true. And I don't have an easy time either!

During this dialogue, a GENTLEMAN *has turned up in front of Shen Te's house, and has whistled several times. Each time* WONG *has given a start.*

THIRD GOD *(to* WONG, *softly)*: Psst! I think he's gone now.

WONG *(confused and surprised)*: Ye-e-es.

The GENTLEMAN *has left now, and* SHEN TE *has come down to the street.*

SHEN TE *(softly)*: Wong!

Getting no answer, she goes off down the street. WONG *arrives just too late, forgetting his carrying pole.*

WONG *(softly)*: Shen Te! Shen Te! *(To himself)* So she's gone off to earn the rent. Oh dear, I can't go to the gods *again* with no room to offer them. Having failed in the service of the gods, I shall run to my den in the sewer pipe down by the river and hide from their sight!

He rushes off. SHEN TE *returns, looking for him, but finding the* GODS. *She stops in confusion.*

SHEN TE: You are the illustrious ones? My name is Shen Te. It would please me very much if my simple room could be of use to you.

THIRD GOD: Where is the water seller, Miss... Shen Te?

SHEN TE: I missed him, somehow.

FIRST GOD: Oh, he probably thought you weren't coming, and was afraid of telling us.

THIRD GOD (*picking up the carrying pole*): We'll leave this with you. He'll be needing it.

Led by SHEN TE, *they go into the house. It grows dark, then light. Dawn. Again escorted by* SHEN TE, *who leads them through the half-light with a little lamp, the* GODS *take their leave.*

FIRST GOD: Thank you, thank you, dear Shen Te, for your elegant hospitality! We shall not forget! And give our thanks to the water seller — he showed us a good human being.

SHEN TE: Oh, *I'm* not good. Let me tell you something: when Wong asked me to put you up, I hesitated.

FIRST GOD: It's all right to hesitate if you then go ahead! And in giving us that room you did much more than you knew. You proved that good people still exist, a point that has been disputed of late — even in heaven. Farewell!

SECOND GOD: Farewell!

THIRD GOD: Farewell!

SHEN TE: Stop, illustrious ones! I'm not sure you're right. I'd like to be good, it's true, but there's the rent to pay. And that's not all: I sell myself for a living. Even so I can't make ends meet, there's too much competition. I'd like to honor my father and mother and speak nothing but the truth and not covet my neighbor's house. I should love to stay with one man. But how? How is it done? Even breaking a few of your commandments, I hardly manage.

FIRST GOD (*clearing his throat*): These thoughts are but, um, the misgivings of an unusually good woman!

THIRD GOD: Good-bye, Shen Te! Give our regards to the water seller!

SECOND GOD: And above all: be good! Farewell!

FIRST GOD: Farewell!

THIRD GOD: Farewell!

They start to wave good-bye.

SHEN TE: But everything is so expensive, I don't feel sure I can do it!

SECOND GOD: That's not in our sphere. We never meddle with economics.

THIRD GOD: One moment. *(They stop.)* Isn't it true she might do better if she had more money?

SECOND GOD: Come, come! How could we ever account for it Up Above?

FIRST GOD: Oh, there are ways. *(They put their heads together and confer in dumb show. To* SHEN TE, *with embarrassment)* As you say you can't pay your rent, well, um, we're not paupers, so of course we *insist* on paying for our room. *(Awkwardly thrusting money into her hands)* There! *(Quickly)* But don't tell anyone! The incident is open to misinterpretation.

SECOND GOD: It certainly is!

FIRST GOD *(defensively)*: But there's no law against it! It was never decreed that a god mustn't pay hotel bills!

The GODS *leave.*

1

A small tobacco shop. The shop is not as yet completely furnished and hasn't started doing business.

SHEN TE *(to the audience)*: It's three days now since the gods left. When they said they wanted to pay for the room, I looked down at my hand, and there was more than a thousand silver dollars! I bought a tobacco shop with the money, and moved in yesterday. I don't own the building, of course, but I can pay the rent, and I hope to do a lot of good here. Beginning with Mrs. Shin, who's just coming across the square with her pot. She had the shop before me, and yesterday she dropped in to ask for rice for her children. *(Enter MRS. SHIN. Both women bow.)* How do you do, Mrs. Shin.

MRS. SHIN: How do you do, Miss Shen Te. You like your new home?

SHEN TE: Indeed, yes. Did your children have a good night?

MRS. SHIN: In that hovel? The youngest is coughing already.

SHEN TE: Oh, dear!

MRS. SHIN: You're going to learn a thing or two in these slums.

SHEN TE: Slums? That's not what you said when you sold me the shop!

MRS. SHIN: Now don't start nagging! Robbing me and my innocent children of their home and then calling it a slum! That's the limit!

(She weeps.)

SHEN TE *(tactfully)*: I'll get your rice.

MRS. SHIN: And a little cash while you're at it.

SHEN TE: I'm afraid I haven't sold anything yet.

MRS. SHIN *(screeching)*: I've got to have it. Strip the clothes from my back and then cut my throat, will you? I know what I'll do: I'll dump my children on your doorstep! *(She snatches the pot out of* SHEN TE'S *hands.)*

SHEN TE: Please don't be angry. You'll spill the rice.

Enter an elderly HUSBAND *and* WIFE *with their shabbily dressed* NEPHEW.

WIFE: Shen Te, dear! You've come into money, they tell me. And we haven't a roof over our heads! A tobacco shop. We had one too. But it's gone. Could we spend the night here, do you think?

NEPHEW *(appraising the shop)*: Not bad!

WIFE: He's our nephew. We're inseparable!

MRS. SHIN: And who are these . . . ladies and gentlemen?

SHEN TE: They put me up when I first came in from the country. *(To the audience)* Of course, when my small purse was empty, they put me out on the street, and they may be afraid I'll do the same to them. *(To the newcomers, kindly)* Come in, and welcome, though I've only one little room for you — it's behind the shop.

HUSBAND: That'll do. Don't worry.

WIFE *(bringing* SHEN TE *some tea)*: We'll stay over here, so we won't be in your way. Did you make it a tobacco shop in memory of your first real home? We can certainly give you a hint or two! That's one reason we came.

MRS. SHIN (*to* SHEN TE): Very nice! As long as you have a few customers too!

HUSBAND: Sh! A customer!

Enter an UNEMPLOYED MAN, *in rags.*

UNEMPLOYED MAN: Excuse me. I'm unemployed.

MRS. SHIN *laughs.*

SHEN TE: Can I help you?

UNEMPLOYED MAN: Have you any damaged cigarettes? I thought there might be some damage when you're unpacking.

WIFE: What nerve, begging for tobacco! (*Rhetorically*) Why don't they ask for bread?

UNEMPLOYED MAN: Bread is expensive. One cigarette butt and I'll be a new man.

SHEN TE (*giving him cigarettes*): That's very important — to be a new man. You'll be my first customer and bring me luck.

The UNEMPLOYED MAN *quickly lights a cigarette, inhales, and goes off, coughing.*

WIFE: Was that right, Shen Te, dear?

MRS. SHIN: If this is the opening of a shop, you can hold the closing at the end of the week.

HUSBAND: I bet he had money on him.

SHEN TE: Oh, no, he said he hadn't!

NEPHEW: How d'you know he wasn't lying?

SHEN TE (*angrily*): How do you know he was?

WIFE (*wagging her head*): You're too good, Shen Te, dear. If you're going to keep this shop, you'll have to learn to say no.

HUSBAND: Tell them the place isn't yours to dispose of. Belongs to . . . some relative who insists on all accounts being strictly in order . . .

MRS. SHIN: That's right! What do you think you are — a philanthropist?

SHEN TE (*laughing*): Very well, suppose I ask you for my rice back, Mrs. Shin?

WIFE (*combatively, at* MRS. SHIN): So that's *her* rice?
Enter the CARPENTER, *a small man.*

MRS. SHIN (*who, at the sight of him, starts to hurry away*): See you tomorrow, Miss Shen Te! (*Exit* MRS. SHIN.)

CARPENTER: Mrs. Shin, it's you I want!

WIFE (*to* SHEN TE): Has she some claim on you?

SHEN TE: She's hungry. That's a claim.

CARPENTER: Are you the new tenant? And filling up the shelves already? Well, they're not yours till they're paid for, ma'am. I'm the carpenter, so I should know.

SHEN TE: I took the shop "furnishings included."

CARPENTER: You're in league with that Mrs. Shin, of course. All right. I demand my hundred silver dollars.

SHEN TE: I'm afraid I haven't got a hundred silver dollars.

CARPENTER: Then you'll find it. Or I'll have you arrested.

WIFE (*whispering to* SHEN TE): That relative: make it a cousin.

SHEN TE: Can't it wait till next month?

CARPENTER: No!

SHEN TE: Be a little patient, Mr. Carpenter, I can't settle all claims at once.

CARPENTER: Who's patient with me? (*He grabs a shelf from the wall.*) Pay up — or I'll take the shelves back!

WIFE: Shen Te! Dear! Why don't you let your… cousin settle this affair? (*To* CARPENTER) Put your claim in writing. Shen Te's cousin will see you get paid.

CARPENTER (*derisively*): Cousin, eh?

HUSBAND: Cousin, yes.

CARPENTER: I know these cousins!

NEPHEW: Don't be silly. He's a personal friend of mine.

HUSBAND: What a man! Sharp as a razor!

CARPENTER: All right. I'll put my claim in writing. (*Puts shelf on floor, sits on it, writes out bill.*)

WIFE (*to* SHEN TE): He'd tear the dress off your back to get his shelves. Never recognize a claim! That's my motto.

SHEN TE: He's done a job, and wants something in return. It's shameful that I can't give it to him. What will the gods say?

HUSBAND: You did your bit when you took *us* in.

Enter the BROTHER, *limping, and the* SISTER-IN-LAW, *pregnant.*

BROTHER (*to* HUSBAND *and* WIFE): So this is where you're hiding out! There's family feeling for you! Leaving us on the corner!

WIFE (*embarrassed, to* SHEN TE): It's my brother and his wife. *(To them)* Now stop grumbling, and sit quietly in that corner. (*To* SHEN TE) It can't be helped. She's in her fifth month.

SHEN TE: Oh yes. Welcome!

WIFE (*to the couple*): Say thank you. *(They mutter something.)* The cups are there. (*To* SHEN TE) Lucky you bought this shop when you did!

SHEN TE (*laughing and bringing tea*): Lucky indeed!

Enter MRS. MI TZU, *the landlady.*

MRS. MI TZU: Miss Shen Te? I am Mrs. Mi Tzu, your landlady. I hope our relationship will be a happy one. I like to think I give my tenants modern, personalized service. Here is your lease. *(To the others, as* SHEN TE *reads the lease)* There's nothing like the opening of a little shop, is there? A moment of true beauty! *(She is looking around.)* Not very much on the shelves, of course. But everything in the gods' good time! Where are your references, Miss Shen Te?

SHEN TE: Do I *have* to have references?

MRS. MI TZU: After all, I haven't a notion who you are!

HUSBAND: Oh, *we'd* be glad to vouch for Miss Shen Te! We'd go through fire for her!

MRS. MI TZU: And who may *you* be?

HUSBAND (*stammering*): Ma Fu, tobacco dealer.

MRS. MI TZU: Where is your shop, Mr. . . . . Ma Fu?

HUSBAND: Well, um, I haven't got a shop — I've just sold it.

MRS. MI TZU: I see. (*To* SHEN TE) Is there no one else that knows you?

WIFE (*whispering to* SHEN TE): Your cousin! Your cousin!

MRS. MI TZU: This is a respectable house, Miss Shen Te. I never sign a lease without certain assurances.

SHEN TE (*slowly, her eyes downcast*): I have . . . a cousin.

MRS. MI TZU: On the square? Let's go over and see him. What does he do?

SHEN TE (*as before*): He lives . . . in another city.

WIFE (*prompting*): Didn't you say he was in Shung?

SHEN TE: That's right. Shung.

HUSBAND (*prompting*): I had his name on the tip of my tongue. Mr. . . .

SHEN TE (*with an effort*): Mr. . . . Shui . . . Ta.

HUSBAND: That's it! Tall, skinny fellow!

SHEN TE: Shui Ta!

NEPHEW (*to* CARPENTER): *You* were in touch with him, weren't you? About the shelves?

CARPENTER (*surlily*): Give him this bill. (*He hands it over.*) I'll be back in the morning. (*Exit* CARPENTER.)

NEPHEW (*calling after him, but with his eyes on* MRS. MI TZU): Don't worry! Mr. Shui Ta pays on the nail!

MRS. MI TZU (*looking closely at* SHEN TE.): I'll be happy to make his acquaintance, Miss Shen Te. (*Exit* MRS. MI TZU.) *Pause.*

WIFE: By tomorrow morning she'll know more about you than you do yourself.

SISTER-IN-LAW (*to* NEPHEW): This thing isn't built to last. *Enter* GRANDFATHER.

WIFE: It's Grandfather! (*To* SHEN TE) Such a good old soul! *The* BOY *enters.*

BOY (*over his shoulder*): Here they are!

WIFE: And the boy, how he's grown! But he always could eat enough for ten.

Enter the NIECE.

WIFE (*to* SHEN TE): Our little niece from the country. There are more of us now than in your time. The less we had, the more there were of us; the more there were of us, the less we had. Give me the key. We must protect ourselves from unwanted guests. *(She takes the key and locks the door.)* Just make yourself at home. I'll light the little lamp.

NEPHEW *(a big joke)*: I hope her cousin doesn't drop in tonight! The strict Mr. Shui Ta!

SISTER-IN-LAW *laughs.*

BROTHER *(reaching for a cigarette)*: One cigarette more or less . . .

HUSBAND: One cigarette more or less.

They pile into the cigarettes. The BROTHER *hands a jug of wine round.*

NEPHEW: Mr. Shui Ta'll pay for it!

GRANDFATHER *(gravely, to* SHEN TE): How do you do?

SHEN TE, *a little taken aback by the belatedness of the greeting, bows. She has the carpenter's bill in one hand, the landlady's lease in the other.*

WIFE: How about a bit of song? To keep Shen Te's spirits up?

NEPHEW: Good idea. Grandfather: you start!

SONG OF THE SMOKE

GRANDFATHER:

>I used to think (before old age beset me)
>>That brains could fill the pantry of the poor.
>But where did all my cerebration get me?
>I'm just as hungry as I was before.
>>So what's the use?
>>>See the smoke float free
>>Into ever colder coldness!
>>>It's the same with me.

HUSBAND:

> The straight and narrow path leads to disaster
> And so the crooked path I tried to tread.
> That got me to disaster even faster.
> (They say we shall be happy when we're dead.)
> So what's the use?
>> See the smoke float free
> Into ever colder coldness!
>> It's the same with me.

NIECE:

> You older people, full of expectation,
> At any moment now you'll walk the plank!
> The future's for the younger generation!
> Yes, even if that future is a blank.
> So what's the use?
>> See the smoke float free
> Into ever colder coldness!
>> It's the same with me.

NEPHEW (*to the* BROTHER): Where'd you get that wine?

SISTER-IN-LAW (*answering for the* BROTHER): He pawned the sack of tobacco.

HUSBAND (*stepping in*): What? That tobacco was all we had to fall back on! You pig!

BROTHER: *You'd* call a man a pig because your wife was frigid! Did you refuse to drink it?
They fight. The shelves fall over.

SHEN TE (*imploringly*): Oh don't! Don't break everything! Take it, take it all, but don't destroy a gift from the gods!

WIFE (*disparagingly*): This shop isn't big enough. I should never have mentioned it to Uncle and the others. When *they* arrive, it's going to be disgustingly overcrowded.

SISTER-IN-LAW: And did you hear our gracious hostess? She cools off quick!
Voices outside. Knocking at the door.

UNCLE'S VOICE: Open the door!

WIFE: Uncle? Is that you, Uncle?

UNCLE'S VOICE: Certainly, it's me. Auntie says to tell you she'll have the children here in ten minutes.

WIFE (*to* SHEN TE): I'll have to let him in.

SHEN TE (*who scarcely hears her*):
The little lifeboat is swiftly sent down.
Too many men too greedily
Hold on to it as they drown.

Wong's den in a sewer pipe.

WONG *(crouching there)*: All quiet! It's four days now since I left the city. The gods passed this way on the second day. I heard their steps on the bridge over there. They must be a long way off by this time, so I'm safe. *(Breathing a sigh of relief, he curls up and goes to sleep. In his dream the pipe becomes transparent, and the* GODS *appear. Raising an arm, as if in self-defense)* I know, I know, illustrious ones! I found no one to give you a room — not in all Setzuan! There, it's out. Please continue on your way!

FIRST GOD *(mildly)*: But you did find someone. Someone who took us in for the night, watched over us in our sleep, and in the early morning lighted us down to the street with a lamp.

WONG: It was . . . Shen Te that took you in?

THIRD GOD: Who else?

WONG: And I ran away! "She isn't coming," I thought, "she just can't afford it."

GODS *(singing)*:

> O you feeble, well-intentioned, and yet feeble chap
> Where there's need the fellow thinks there is no goodness!
> When there's danger he thinks courage starts to ebb away!
> Some people only see the seamy side!
> What hasty judgment! What premature desperation!

WONG: I'm *very* ashamed, illustrious ones.

FIRST GOD: Do us a favor, water seller. Go back to Setzuan. Find Shen Te, and give us a report on her. We hear that she's come into a little money. Show interest in her goodness — for no one can be good for long if goodness is not in demand. Meanwhile we shall continue the search, and find other good people. After which, the idle chatter about the impossibility of goodness will stop!

The GODS *vanish.*

2

A knocking.

WIFE: Shen Te! Someone at the door. Where is she anyway?
NEPHEW: She must be getting the breakfast. Mr. Shui Ta will
   pay for it.
   The WIFE *laughs and shuffles to the door. Enter* MR. SHUI TA
   and the CARPENTER.
WIFE: Who is it?
SHUI TA: I am Miss Shen Te's cousin.
WIFE: What?
SHUI TA: My name is Shui Ta.
WIFE: Her cousin?
NEPHEW: Her cousin?
NIECE: But that was a joke. She hasn't got a cousin.
HUSBAND: So early in the morning?
BROTHER: What's all the noise?
SISTER-IN-LAW: This fellow says he's her cousin.
BROTHER: Tell him to prove it.
NEPHEW: Right. If you're Shen Te's cousin, prove it by getting
   the breakfast.

SHUI TA (*whose regime begins as he puts out the lamp to save oil; loudly, to all present, asleep or awake*): Would you all please get dressed! Customers will be coming! I wish to open my shop!

HUSBAND: *Your* shop! Doesn't it belong to our good friend Shen Te?

SHUI TA *shakes his head.*

SISTER-IN-LAW: So we've been cheated. Where *is* the little liar?

SHUI TA: Miss Shen Te has been delayed. She wishes me to tell you there will be nothing she can do — now I am here.

WIFE (*bowled over*): I thought she was good!

NEPHEW: Do you have to believe *him*?

HUSBAND: I don't.

NEPHEW: Then do something.

HUSBAND: Certainly! I'll send out a search party at once. You, you, you, and you, go out and look for Shen Te. (*As the* GRANDFATHER *rises and makes for the door*) Not you, Grandfather, you and I will hold the fort.

SHUI TA: You won't find Miss Shen Te. She has suspended her hospitable activity for an unlimited period. There are too many of you. She asked me to say: this is a tobacco shop, not a gold mine.

HUSBAND: Shen Te never said a thing like that. Boy, food! There's a bakery on the corner. Stuff your shirt full when they're not looking!

SISTER-IN-LAW: Don't overlook the raspberry tarts.

HUSBAND: And don't let the policeman see you.

The BOY *leaves.*

SHUI TA: Don't you depend on this shop now? Then why give it a bad name by stealing from the bakery?

NEPHEW: Don't listen to him. Let's find Shen Te. She'll give him a piece of her mind.

SISTER-IN-LAW: Don't forget to leave us some breakfast.

BROTHER, SISTER-IN-LAW, *and* NEPHEW *leave.*

SHUI TA (*to the* CARPENTER): You see, Mr. Carpenter, nothing has changed since the poet, eleven hundred years ago, penned these lines:

> A governor was asked what was needed
> To save the freezing people in the city.
> He replied:
> "A blanket ten thousand feet long
> To cover the city and all its suburbs."

He starts to tidy up the shop.

CARPENTER: Your cousin owes me money. I've got witnesses. For the shelves.

SHUI TA: Yes, I have your bill. (*He takes it out of his pocket.*) Isn't a hundred silver dollars rather a lot?

CARPENTER: No deductions! I have a wife and children.

SHUI TA: How many children?

CARPENTER: Three.

SHUI TA: I'll make you an offer. Twenty silver dollars.

The HUSBAND *laughs.*

CARPENTER: You're crazy. Those shelves are real walnut.

SHUI TA: Very well. Take them away.

CARPENTER: What?

SHUI TA: They cost too much. Please take them away.

WIFE: Not bad! (*And she, too, is laughing.*)

CARPENTER (*a little bewildered*): Call Shen Te, someone! (*To* SHUI TA) She's *good!*

SHUI TA: Certainly. She's ruined.

CARPENTER (*provoked into taking some of the shelves*): All right, you can keep your tobacco on the floor.

SHUI TA (*to the* HUSBAND): Help him with the shelves.

HUSBAND (*grins and carries one shelf over to the door where the* CARPENTER *now is*): Good-bye, shelves!

CARPENTER (*to the* HUSBAND): You dog! You want my family to starve?

SHUI TA: I repeat my offer. I have no desire to keep my tobacco on the floor. Twenty silver dollars.

CARPENTER (*with desperate aggressiveness*): One hundred!

SHUI TA *shows indifference, looks through the window. The* HUSBAND *picks up several shelves.*

CARPENTER (*to* HUSBAND): You needn't smash them against the doorpost, you idiot! (*To* SHUI TA) These shelves were made to measure. They're no use anywhere else!

SHUI TA: Precisely.

The WIFE *squeals with pleasure.*

CARPENTER (*giving up, sullenly*): Take the shelves. Pay what you want to pay.

SHUI TA (*smoothly*): Twenty silver dollars.

He places two large coins on the table. The CARPENTER *picks them up.*

HUSBAND (*brings the shelves back in*): And quite enough too!

CARPENTER (*slinking off*): Quite enough to get drunk on.

HUSBAND (*happily*): Well, we got rid of *him*!

WIFE (*weeping with fun, gives a rendition of the dialogue just spoken*): "Real walnut," says he. "Very well, take them away," says his lordship. "I have three children," says he. "Twenty silver dollars," says his lordship. "They're no use anywhere else," says he. "Pre-cisely," said his lordship! (*She dissolves into shrieks of merriment.*)

SHUI TA: And now: go!

HUSBAND: What's that?

SHUI TA: You're thieves, parasites. I'm giving you this chance. Go!

HUSBAND (*summoning all his ancestral dignity*): That sort deserves no answer. Besides, one should never shout on an empty stomach.

WIFE: Where's that boy?

SHUI TA: Exactly. The boy. I want no stolen goods in this shop. (*Very loudly*) I strongly advise you to leave! (*But they remain seated, noses in the air. Quietly*) As you wish. (SHUI TA *goes to the door. A* POLICEMAN *appears.* SHUI TA *bows.*) I am addressing the officer in charge of this precinct?

POLICEMAN: That's right, Mr., um, what was the name, sir?

SHUI TA: Mr. Shui Ta.

POLICEMAN: Yes, of course, sir.

They exchange a smile.

SHUI TA: Nice weather we're having.

POLICEMAN: A little on the warm side, sir.

SHUI TA: Oh, a little on the warm side.

HUSBAND (*whispering to the* WIFE): If he keeps it up till the boy's back, we're done for. (*Tries to signal* SHUI TA.)

SHUI TA (*ignoring the signal*): Weather, of course, is one thing indoors, another out on the dusty street!

POLICEMAN: Oh, quite another, sir!

WIFE (*to the* HUSBAND): It's all right as long as he's standing in the doorway — the boy will see him.

SHUI TA: Step inside for a moment! It's quite cool indoors. My cousin and I have just opened the place. And we attach the greatest importance to being on good terms and the, um, authorities.

POLICEMAN (*entering*): Thank you, Mr. Shui Ta. It *is* cool!

HUSBAND (*whispering to the* WIFE): And now the boy *won't* see him.

SHUI TA (*showing* HUSBAND *and* WIFE *to the* POLICEMAN): Visitors, I think my cousin knows them. They were just leaving.

HUSBAND (*defeated*): Ye-e-es, we were . . . just leaving.

SHUI TA: I'll tell my cousin you couldn't wait.

Noise from the street. Shouts of "Stop, Thief!"

POLICEMAN: What's that?

The BOY *is in the doorway with cakes and buns and rolls spilling out of his shirt. The* WIFE *signals desperately to him to leave. He gets the idea.*

POLICEMAN: No, you don't! (*He grabs the* BOY *by the collar.*): Where's all this from?

BOY (*vaguely pointing*): Down the street.

POLICEMAN (*grimly*): So that's it. (*Prepares to arrest the* BOY.)

WIFE *(stepping in)*: And *we* knew nothing about it. (*To the* BOY) Nasty little thief!

POLICEMAN *(dryly)*: Can you clarify the situation, Mr. Shui Ta?

SHUI TA *is silent.*

POLICEMAN *(who understands silence)*: Aha. You're all coming with me — to the station.

SHUI TA: I can hardly say how sorry I am that *my* establishment . . .

WIFE: Oh, he saw the boy leave not ten minutes ago!

SHUI TA: And to conceal the theft asked a policeman in?

POLICEMAN: Don't listen to her, Mr. Shui Ta, I'll be happy to relieve you of their presence one and all! *(To all three)* Out! *(He drives them before him.)*

GRANDFATHER *(leaving last, gravely)*: Good morning!

POLICEMAN: Good morning!

SHUI TA, *left alone, continues to tidy up.* MRS. MI TZU *breezes in.*

MRS. MI TZU: *You're* her cousin, are you? Then have the goodness to explain what all this means — police dragging people from a respectable house! By what right does your Miss Shen Te turn my property into a house of assignation? — Well, as you see, I know all!

SHUI TA: Yes. My cousin has the worst possible reputation: that of being poor.

MRS. MI TZU: No sentimental rubbish, Mr. Shui Ta. Your cousin was a common . . .

SHUI TA: Pauper. Let's use the uglier word.

MRS. MI TZU: I'm speaking of her conduct, not her earnings. But there must have *been* earnings, or how did she buy all this? Several elderly gentlemen took care of it, I suppose. I repeat: this is a respectable house! I have tenants who prefer not to live under the same room with such a person.

SHUI TA *(quietly)*: How much do you want?

MRS. MI TZU *(he is ahead of her now)*: I beg your pardon.

SHUI TA: To reassure yourself. To reassure your tenants. How much will it cost?

MRS. MI TZU: You're a cool customer.

SHUI TA *(picking up the lease)*: The rent is high. *(He reads on.)* I assume it's payable by the month?

MRS. MI TZU: Not in her case.

SHUI TA *(looking up)*: What?

MRS. MI TZU: Six months' rent payable in advance. Two hundred silver dollars.

SHUI TA: Six...! Sheer usury! And where am I to find it?

MRS. MI TZU: You should have thought of that before.

SHUI TA: Have you no heart, Mrs. Mi Tzu? It's true Shen Te acted foolishly, being kind to all those people, but she'll improve with time. I'll see to it she does. She'll work her fingers to the bone to pay her rent, and all the time be as quiet as a mouse, as humble as a fly.

MRS. MI TZU: Her social background...

SHUI TA: Out of the depths! She came out of the depths! And before she'll go back there, she'll work, sacrifice, shrink from nothing.... Such a tenant is worth her weight in gold, Mrs. Mi Tzu.

MRS. MI TZU: It's silver we were talking about, Mr. Shui Ta. Two hundred silver dollars or...

Enter the POLICEMAN.

POLICEMAN: Am I intruding, Mr. Shui Ta?

MRS. MI TZU: This tobacco shop is well known to the police, I see.

POLICEMAN: Mr. Shui Ta has done us a service, Mrs. Mi Tzu. I am here to present our official felicitations!

MRS. MI TZU: That means less than nothing to me, sir. Mr. Shui Ta, all I can say is: I hope your cousin will find my terms acceptable. Good day, gentlemen. *(Exit.)*

SHUI TA: Good day, ma'am.

Pause.

POLICEMAN: Mrs. Mi Tzu a bit of a stumbling block, sir?

SHUI TA: She wants six months' rent in advance.

POLICEMAN: And you haven't got it, eh? (SHUI TA *is silent.*) But surely you can get it, sir? A man like you?

SHUI TA: What about a woman like Shen Te?

POLICEMAN: You're not staying, sir?

SHUI TA: No, and I won't be back. Do you smoke?

POLICEMAN (*taking two cigars, and placing them both in his pocket*): Thank you, sir — I see your point. Miss Shen Te — let's mince no words — Miss Shen Te lived by selling herself. "What else could she have done?" you ask. "How else was she to pay the rent?" True. But the fact remains, Mr. Shui Ta, it is not respectable. Why not? A very deep question. But, in the first place, love — love isn't bought and sold like cigars, Mr. Shui Ta. In the second place, it isn't respectable to go waltzing off with someone that's paying his way, so to speak — it must be for love! Thirdly and lastly, as the proverb has it: not for a handful of rice but for love! (*Pause. He is thinking hard.*) "Well," you may say, "and what good is all this wisdom if the milk's already spilt?" Miss Shen Te is what she is. Is *where* she is. We have to face the fact that if she doesn't get hold of six months' rent pronto, she'll be back on the streets. The question then as I see it — everything in this world is a matter of opinion — the question as I see it is: *how* is she to get hold of the rent? How? Mr. Shui Ta: I don't know. (*Pause.*) I take that back, sir. It's just come to me. A husband. We must find her a husband!

Enter a little OLD WOMAN.

OLD WOMAN: A good cheap cigar for my husband, we'll have been married forty years tomorrow and we're having a little celebration.

SHUI TA: Forty years? And you still want to celebrate?

OLD WOMAN: As much as we can afford to. We have the carpet shop across the square. We'll be good neighbors, I hope?

SHUI TA: I hope so too.

POLICEMAN (*who keeps making discoveries*): Mr. Shui Ta, you know what we need? We need capital. And how do we acquire capital? We get married.

SHUI TA (*to* OLD WOMAN): I'm afraid I've been pestering this gentleman with my personal worries.

POLICEMAN (*lyrically*): We can't pay six months' rent, so what do we do? We marry money.

SHUI TA: That might not be easy.

POLICEMAN: Oh, I don't know. She's a good match. Has a nice, growing business. (*To the* OLD WOMAN) What do you think?

OLD WOMAN (*undecided*): Well—

POLICEMAN: Should she put an ad in the paper?

OLD WOMAN (*not eager to commit herself*): Well, if *she* agrees—

POLICEMAN: I'll write it for her. *You* lend us a hand, and *we* write an ad for you! (*He chuckles away to himself, takes out his notebook, wets the stump of a pencil between his lips, and writes away.*)

SHUI TA (*slowly*): Not a bad idea.

POLICEMAN: "What . . . *respectable* . . . man . . . with small capital . . . widower . . . not   excluded . . . desires . . . marriage . . . into flourishing . . . tobacco shop?" And now let's add: "Am . . . pretty . . ." No! . . . "Prepossessing appearance."

SHUI TA: If you don't think that's an exaggeration?

OLD WOMAN: Oh, not a bit. I've seen her.

The POLICEMAN *tears the page out of his notebook, and hands it over to* SHUI TA.

SHUI TA (*with horror in his voice*): How much luck we need to keep our heads above water! How many ideas! How many friends! (*To the* POLICEMAN) Thank you, sir, I think I see my way clear.

3

Evening in the municipal park. Noise of a plane overhead. YANG
SUN, *a young man in rags, is following the plane with his eyes:
one can tell that the machine is describing a curve above the park.*
YANG SUN *then takes a rope out of his pocket, looking anxiously
about him as he does so. He moves toward a large willow. Enter*
TWO PROSTITUTES, *one old, the other the* NIECE *whom we
have already met.*

NIECE: Hello. Coming with me?
YANG SUN *(taken aback)*: If you'd like to buy me a dinner.
OLD WHORE: Buy you a dinner! (*To the* NIECE) Oh, we know
    him — it's the unemployed pilot. Waste no time on him!
NIECE: But he's the only man left in the park. And it's going
    to rain.
OLD WHORE: Oh, how do you know?
    And they pass by. YANG SUN *again looks about him, again
    takes his rope, and this time throws it round a branch of the
    willow tree. Again he is interrupted. It is the* TWO PROSTI-
    TUTES *returning — and in such a hurry they don't notice him.*

NIECE: It's going to pour!

Enter SHEN TE.

OLD WHORE: There's that *gorgon* Shen Te! That *drove* your family out into the cold!

NIECE: It wasn't her. It was that cousin of hers. She offered to pay for the cakes. I've nothing against her.

OLD WHORE: I have, though. *(So that* SHEN TE *can hear)* Now where could the little lady be off to? She may be rich now but that won't stop her snatching our young men, will it?

SHEN TE: I'm going to the tearoom by the pond.

NIECE: Is it true what they say? You're marrying a widower — with three children?

SHEN TE: Yes, I'm just going to see him.

YANG SUN *(his patience at breaking point)*: Move on there! This is a park, not a whorehouse!

OLD WHORE: Shut your mouth!

But the TWO PROSTITUTES *leave.*

YANG SUN: Even in the farthest corner of the park, even when it's raining, you can't get rid of them! *(He spits.)*

SHEN TE *(overhearing this)*: And what right have you to scold them?

(But at this point she sees the rope.) Oh!

YANG SUN: Well, what are you staring at?

SHEN TE: That rope. What is it for?

YANG SUN: Think! Think! I haven't a penny. Even if I had, I wouldn't spend it on you. I'd buy a drink of water.

The rain starts.

SHEN TE *(still looking at the rope)*: What is the rope for? You mustn't!

YANG SUN: What's it to you? Clear out!

SHEN TE *(irrelevantly)*: It's raining.

YANG SUN: Well, don't try to come under this tree.

SHEN TE: Oh, no. *(She stays in the rain.)*

YANG SUN: Now go away. *(Pause.)* For one thing, I don't like your looks, you're bowlegged.

SHEN TE (*indignantly*): That's not true!

YANG SUN: Well, don't show 'em to me. Look, it's raining. You better come under this tree.

Slowly, she takes shelter under the tree.

SHEN TE: Why did you want to do it?

YANG SUN: You really want to know? (*Pause.*) To get rid of you! (*Pause.*) You know what a flyer is?

SHEN TE: Oh yes, I've met a lot of pilots. At the tearoom.

YANG SUN: You call *them* flyers? Think they know what a machine is? Just 'cause they have leather helmets? They gave the airfield director a bribe, that's the way *those* fellows got up in the air! Try one of them out sometime. "Go up to two thousand feet," tell him, "then let it fall, then pick it up again with a flick of the wrist at the last moment." Know what he'll say to that? "It's not in my contract." Then again, there's the landing problem. It's like landing on your own backside. It's no different, planes are human. Those fools don't understand. (*Pause.*) And I'm the biggest fool for reading the book on flying in the Peking school and skipping the page where it says: "We've got enough flyers and we don't need you." I'm a mail pilot with no mail. You understand that?

SHEN TE (*shyly*): Yes. I do.

YANG SUN: No, you don't. You'd never understand that.

SHEN TE: When we were little we had a crane with a broken wing. He made friends with us and was very good-natured about our jokes. He would strut along behind us and call out to stop us going too fast for him. But every spring and autumn when the cranes flew over the villages in great swarms, he got quite restless. (*Pause.*) I understand that.

She bursts out crying.

YANG SUN: Don't!

SHEN TE (*quieting down*): No.

YANG SUN: It's bad for the complexion.

SHEN TE (*sniffing*): I've stopped.

*She dries her tears on her big sleeve. Leaning against the tree,
but not looking at her, he reaches for her face.*

YANG SUN: You can't even wipe your own face. *(He is wiping
it for her with his handkerchief. Pause.)*

SHEN TE *(still sobbing)*: I don't know *anything*!

YANG SUN: You interrupted me! What for?

SHEN TE: It's such a rainy day. You only wanted to do . . . *that*
because it's such a rainy day. *(To the audience)*

> In our country
> The evenings should never be somber
> High bridges over rivers
> The gray hour between night and morning
> And the long, long winter:
> Such things are dangerous
> For, with all the misery,
> A very little is enough
> And men throw away an unbearable life.

Pause.

YANG SUN: Talk about yourself for a change.

SHEN TE: What about me? I have a shop.

YANG SUN *(incredulous)*: You have a shop, have you? Never
thought of walking the streets?

SHEN TE: I did walk the streets. Now I have a shop.

YANG SUN *(ironically)*: A gift of the gods, I suppose!

SHEN TE: How did you know?

YANG SUN *(even more ironical)*: One fine evening the gods
turned up saying: here's some money!

SHEN TE *(quickly)*: One fine morning.

YANG SUN *(fed up)*: This isn't much of an entertainment.

Pause.

SHEN TE: I can play the zither a little. *(Pause.)* And I can mim-
ic men. *(Pause.)* I got the shop, so the first thing I did was
to give my zither away. I can be as stupid as a fish now, I
said to myself, and it won't matter.

I'm rich now, I said
I walk alone, I sleep alone.
For a whole year, I said
I'll have nothing to do with a man.

YANG SUN: And now you're marrying one! The one at the tea-room by the pond?

SHEN TE *is silent.*

YANG SUN: What do you know about love?

SHEN TE: Everything.

YANG SUN: Nothing. *(Pause.)* Or d'you just mean you enjoyed it?

SHEN TE: No.

YANG SUN *(again without turning to look at her, he strokes her cheek with his hand)*: You like that?

SHEN TE: Yes.

YANG SUN *(breaking off)*: You're easily satisfied, I must say. *(Pause.)* What a town!

SHEN TE: You have no friends?

YANG SUN *(defensively)*: Yes, I have! *(Change of tone.)* But they don't want to hear I'm still unemployed. "What?" they ask. "Is there still water in the sea?" You have friends?

SHEN TE *(hesitating)*: Just a . . . cousin.

YANG SUN: Watch him carefully.

SHEN TE: He only came once. Then he went away. He won't be back. (YANG SUN *is looking away.*) But to be without hope, they say, is to be without goodness!
Pause.

YANG SUN: Go on talking. A voice is a voice.

SHEN TE: Once, when I was a little girl, I fell, with a load of brushwood. An old man picked me up. He gave me a penny too. Isn't it funny how people who don't have very much like to give some of it away? They must like to show what they can do, and how could they show it better than by being kind? Being wicked is just like being clumsy. When we sing a song, or build a machine, or plant some rice, we're being kind. You're kind.

YANG SUN: You make it sound easy.

SHEN TE: Oh, no. *(Little pause.)* Oh! A drop of rain!

YANG SUN: Where'd you feel it?

SHEN TE: Between the eyes.

YANG SUN: Near the right eye? Or the left?

SHEN TE: Near the left eye.

YANG SUN: Oh, good. *(He is getting sleepy.)* So you're through with men, eh?

SHEN TE *(with a smile)*: But I'm not bowlegged.

YANG SUN: Perhaps not.

SHEN TE: Definitely not.

Pause.

YANG SUN *(leaning wearily against the willow)*: I haven't had a drop to drink all day, I haven't eaten anything for *two* days. I couldn't love you if I tried.

Pause.

SHEN TE: I like it in the rain.

Enter WONG *the water seller, singing.*

THE SONG OF THE WATER SELLER IN THE RAIN

"Buy my water," I am yelling
And my fury restraining
For no water I'm selling
'Cause it's raining, 'cause it's raining!
　　I keep yelling: "Buy my water!"
　　But no one's buying
　　Athirst and dying
　　And drinking and paying!
　　Buy water!
　　Buy water, you dogs!

Nice to dream of lovely weather!
Think of all the consternation
Were there no precipitation
Half a dozen years together!
   Can't you hear them shrieking: "Water!"
   Pretending they adore me?
   They all would go down on their knees before me!
   Down on your knees!
   Go down on your knees, you dogs!

What are lawns and hedges thinking?
What are fields and forests saying?
"At the cloud's breast we are drinking!
And we've no idea who's paying!"
   I keep yelling: "Buy my water!"
   But no one's buying
   Athirst and dying
   And drinking and paying!
   Buy water!
   Buy water, you dogs!

The rain has stopped now. SHEN TE *sees* WONG *and runs toward him.*

SHEN TE: Wong! You're back! Your carrying pole's at the shop.

WONG: Oh, thank you, Shen Te. And how is life treating *you*?

SHEN TE: I've just met a brave and clever man. And I want to buy him a cup of your water.

WONG *(bitterly)*: Throw back your head and open your mouth and you'll have all the water you need—

SHEN TE *(tenderly)*:
I want *your* water, Wong
The water that has tired you so
The water that you carried all this way
The water that is hard to sell because it's been raining.
I need it for the young man over there—he's a flyer!
A flyer is a bold man:

Braving the storms
In company with the clouds
He crosses the heavens
And brings to friends in faraway lands
The friendly mail!

She pays WONG, *and runs over to* YANG SUN *with the cup.*
But YANG SUN *is fast asleep.*

SHEN TE *(calling to* WONG, *with a laugh)*: He's fallen asleep!
Despair and rain and I have worn him out!

Wong's den. The sewer pipe is transparent, and the GODS *again appear to* WONG *in a dream.*

WONG *(radiant)*: I've seen her, illustrious ones! And she hasn't changed!

FIRST GOD: That's good to hear.

WONG: She loves someone.

FIRST GOD: Let's hope the experience gives her the strength to stay good!

WONG: It does. She's doing good deeds all the time.

FIRST GOD: Ah? What sort? What sort of good deeds, Wong?

WONG: Well, she has a kind word for everybody.

FIRST GOD *(eagerly)*: And then?

WONG: Hardly anyone leaves her shop without tobacco in his pocket — even if he can't pay for it.

FIRST GOD: Not bad at all. Next?

WONG: She's putting up a family of eight.

FIRST GOD *(gleefully, to the* SECOND GOD*)*: Eight! (*To* WONG) And that's not all, of course!

WONG: She bought a cup of water from me even though it was raining.

FIRST GOD: Yes, yes, yes, all these smaller good deeds!

WONG: Even they run into money. A little tobacco shop doesn't make so much.

FIRST GOD *(sententiously)*: A prudent gardener works miracles on the smallest plot.

WONG: She hands out rice every morning. That eats up half her earnings.

FIRST GOD *(a little disappointed)*: Well, as a beginning...

WONG: They call her the Angel of the Slums — whatever the carpenter may say!

FIRST GOD: What's this? A carpenter speaks ill of her?

WONG: Oh, he only says her shelves weren't paid for in full.

SECOND GOD *(who has a bad cold and can't pronounce his n's and m's)*: What's this? Not paying a carpenter? Why was that?

WONG: I suppose she didn't have the money.

SECOND GOD *(severely)*: One pays what one owes, that's in our book of rules! First the letter of the law, then the spirit.

WONG: But it wasn't Shen Te, illustrious ones, it was her cousin. She called *him* in to help.

SECOND GOD: Then her cousin must never darken her threshold again!

WONG: Very well, illustrious ones! But in fairness to Shen Te, let me say that her cousin is a businessman.

FIRST GOD: Perhaps we should inquire what is customary? I find business quite unintelligible. But everybody's doing it. Business! Did the Seven Good Kings do business? Did Kung the Just sell fish?

SECOND GOD: In any case, such a thing must not occur again!
The GODS *start to leave.*

THIRD GOD: Forgive us for taking this tone with you, Wong, we haven't been getting enough sleep. The rich recommend us to the poor, and the poor tell us they haven't enough room.

SECOND GOD: Feeble, feeble, the best of them!

FIRST GOD: No great deeds! No heroic daring!

THIRD GOD: On such a *small* scale!

SECOND GOD: Sincere, yes, but what is actually *achieved?*
One can no longer hear them.

WONG *(calling after them)*: I've thought of something, illustrious
ones: Perhaps you shouldn't ask — too — much — all — at —
once!

4

The square in front of Shen Te's tobacco shop. Besides Shen Te's place, two other shops are seen: the carpet shop and a barber's. Morning. Outside Shen Te's the GRANDFATHER, *the* SISTER-IN-LAW, *the* UNEMPLOYED MAN, *and* MRS. SHIN *stand waiting.*

SISTER-IN-LAW: She's been out all night again.

MRS. SHIN: No sooner did we get rid of that crazy cousin of hers than Shen Te herself starts carrying on! Maybe she does give us an ounce of rice now and then, but can you depend on her? Can you depend on her?

Loud voices from the barber's.

VOICE OF SHU FU: What are you doing in my shop? Get out — at once!

VOICE OF WONG: But sir. They all let me sell . . .

WONG *comes staggering out of the barber's shop pursued by* MR. SHU FU, *the barber, a fat man carrying a heavy curling iron.*

SHU FU: Get out, I said! Pestering my customers with your slimy old water! Get out! Take your cup!

43

He holds out the cup. WONG *reaches out for it.* MR. SHU FU *strikes his hand with the curling iron, which is hot.* WONG *howls.*

SHU FU: You had it coming, my man!

Puffing, he returns to his shop. The UNEMPLOYED MAN *picks up the cup and gives it to* WONG.

UNEMPLOYED MAN: You can report that to the police.

WONG: My hand! It's smashed up!

UNEMPLOYED MAN: Any bones broken?

WONG: I can't move my fingers.

UNEMPLOYED MAN: Sit down. I'll put some water on it.

WONG *sits.*

MRS. SHIN: The water won't cost you anything.

SISTER-IN-LAW: You might have got a bandage from Miss Shen Te till she took to staying out all night. It's a scandal.

MRS. SHIN *(despondently)*: If you ask me, she's forgotten we ever existed!

Enter SHEN TE *down the street, with a dish of rice.*

SHEN TE *(to the audience)*: How wonderful to see Setzuan in the early morning! I always used to stay in bed with my dirty blanket over my head afraid to wake up. This morning I saw the newspapers being delivered by little boys, the streets being washed by strong men, and fresh vegetables coming in from the country on ox carts. It's a long walk from where Yang Sun lives, but I feel lighter at every step. They say you walk on air when you're in love, but it's even better walking on the rough earth, on the hard cement. In the early morning, the old city looks like a great heap of rubbish! Nice, though, with all its little lights. And the sky, so pink, so transparent, before the dust comes and muddies it! What a lot you miss if you never see your city rising from its slumbers like an honest old craftsman pumping his lungs full of air and reaching for his tools, as the poet says! *(Cheerfully, to her waiting guests)* Good morning, everyone, here's your rice! *(Distributing the rice, she comes upon* WONG.) Good morning, Wong,

I'm quite lightheaded today. On my way over, I looked at myself in all the shop windows. I'd love to be beautiful.
She slips into the carpet shop. MR. SHU FU *has just emerged from his shop.*

SHU FU *(to the audience)*: It surprises me how beautiful Miss Shen Te is looking today! I never gave her a passing thought before. But now I've been gazing upon her comely form for exactly three minutes! I begin to suspect I am in love with her. She is overpoweringly attractive! *(Crossly, to* WONG) Be off with you, rascal!
He returns to his shop. SHEN TE *comes back out of the carpet shop with the* OLD MAN, *its proprietor, and his wife—whom we have already met—the* OLD WOMAN. SHEN TE *is wearing a shawl. The* OLD MAN *is holding up a looking glass for her.*

OLD WOMAN: Isn't it lovely? We'll give you a reduction because there's a little hole in it.
SHEN TE *(looking at another shawl on the* OLD WOMAN'S *arm)*: The other one's nice too.
OLD WOMAN *(smiling)*: Too bad there's no hole in that!
SHEN TE: That's right. My shop doesn't make very much.
OLD WOMAN: And your good deeds eat it all up! Be more careful, my dear. . . .
SHEN TE *(trying on the shawl with the hole)*: Just now, I'm lightheaded! Does the color suit me?
OLD WOMAN: You'd better ask a man.
SHEN TE *(to the* OLD MAN): Does the color suit me?
OLD MAN: You'd better ask your young friend.
SHEN TE: I'd like to have your opinion.
OLD MAN: It suits you very well. But wear it this way: the dull side out.
SHEN TE *pays up.*
OLD WOMAN: If you decide you don't like it, you can exchange it. *(She pulls* SHEN TE *to one side.)* Has he got money?
SHEN TE *(with a laugh)*: Yang Sun? Oh, No.
OLD WOMAN: Then how're you going to pay your rent?

SHEN TE: I'd forgotten about that.

OLD WOMAN: And next Monday is the first of the month! Miss Shen Te, I've got something to say to you. After we *(indicating her husband)* got to know you, we had our doubts about that marriage ad. We thought it would be better if you'd let *us* help you. Out of our savings. We reckon we could lend you two hundred silver dollars. We don't need anything in writing—you could pledge us your tobacco stock.

SHEN TE: You're prepared to lend money to a person like me?

OLD WOMAN: It's folks like you that need it. We'd think twice about lending anything to your cousin.

OLD MAN *(coming up)*: All settled, my dear?

SHEN TE: I wish the gods could have heard what your wife was just saying, Mr. Ma. They're looking for good people who're happy—and helping me makes you happy because you know it was love that got me into difficulties!

The OLD COUPLE *smile knowingly at each other.*

OLD MAN: And here's the money, Miss Shen Te.

He hands her an envelope. SHEN TE *takes it. She bows. They bow back. They return to their shop.*

SHEN TE *(holding up her envelope)*: Look, Wong, here's six months' rent! Don't you believe in miracles now? And how do you like my new shawl?

WONG: For the young fellow I saw you with in the park?

SHEN TE *nods.*

MRS. SHIN: Never mind all that. It's time you took a look at his hand!

SHEN TE: Have you hurt your hand?

MRS. SHIN: That barber smashed it with his hot curling iron. Right in front of our eyes.

SHEN TE *(shocked at herself)*: And I never noticed! We must get you to a doctor this minute or who knows what will happen?

UNEMPLOYED MAN: It's not a doctor he should see, it's a judge. He can ask for compensation. The barber's filthy rich.

WONG: You think I have a chance?

MRS. SHIN *(with relish)*: If it's really good and smashed. But is it?

WONG: I think so. It's very swollen. Could I get a pension?

MRS. SHIN: You'd need a witness.

WONG: Well, you saw it. You could all testify.

He looks round. The UNEMPLOYED MAN, *the* GRAND-FATHER, *and the* SISTER-IN-LAW *are all sitting against the wall of the shop eating rice. Their concentration on eating is complete.*

SHEN TE *(to* MRS. SHIN*)*: You saw it yourself.

MRS. SHIN: I want nothing to do with the police. It's against my principles.

SHEN TE *(to* SISTER-IN-LAW*)*: What about you?

SISTER-IN-LAW: Me? I wasn't looking.

SHEN TE *(to the* GRANDFATHER, *coaxingly)*: Grandfather, *you'll* testify, won't you?

SISTER-IN-LAW: And a lot of good that will do. He's simple-minded.

SHEN TE *(to the* UNEMPLOYED MAN*)*: You seem to be the only witness left.

UNEMPLOYED MAN: My testimony would only hurt him. I've been picked up twice for begging.

SHEN TE:

Your brother is assaulted, and you shut your eyes?
He is hit, cries out in pain, and you are silent?
The beast prowls, chooses and seizes his victim, and you say:
"Because we showed no displeasure, he has spared us."
If no one present will be witness, I will. I'll say *I* saw it.

MRS. SHIN *(solemnly)*: The name for that is perjury.

WONG: I don't know if I can accept that. Though maybe I'll have to. *(Looking at his hand)* Is it swollen enough, do you think? The swelling's not going down?

UNEMPLOYED MAN: No, no, the swelling's holding up well.

WONG: Yes. It's *more* swollen if anything. Maybe my wrist is broken after all. I'd better see a judge at once.

Holding his hand very carefully, and fixing his eyes on it, he runs off. MRS. SHIN *goes quickly into the barber's shop.*

UNEMPLOYED MAN *(seeing her)*: She is getting on the right side of Mr. Shu Fu.

SISTER-IN-LAW: You and I can't change the world, Shen Te.

SHEN TE: Go away! Go away all of you! *(The* UNEMPLOYED MAN, *the* SISTER-IN-LAW, *and the* GRANDFATHER *stalk off, eating and sulking. To the audience)*

> They've stopped answering
> They stay put
> They do as they're told
> They don't care
> Nothing can make them look up
> But the smell of food.

Enter MRS. YANG, *Yang Sun's mother, out of breath.*

MRS. YANG: Miss Shen Te. My son has told me everything. I am Mrs. Yang, Sun's mother. Just think. He's got an offer. Of a job as a pilot. A letter has just come. From the director of the airfield in Peking!

SHEN TE: So he can fly again? Isn't that wonderful!

MRS. YANG *(less breathlessly all the time)*: They won't give him the job for nothing. They want five hundred silver dollars.

SHEN TE: We can't let money stand in his way, Mrs. Yang!

MRS. YANG: If only you could help him out!

SHEN TE: I have the shop. I can try! *(She embraces* MRS. YANG.)* I happen to have two hundred with me now. Take it. *(She gives her the old couple's money.)* It was a loan but they said I could repay it with my tobacco stock.

MRS. YANG: And they were calling Sun the Dead Pilot of Setzuan! A friend in need!

SHEN TE: We must find another three hundred.

MRS. YANG: How?

SHEN TE: Let me think. *(Slowly)* I know someone who can help. I didn't want to call on his services again, he's hard and cunning. But a flyer must fly. And I'll make this the last time.

Distant sound of a plane.

MRS. YANG: If the man you mentioned can do it.... Oh, look, there's the morning mail plane, heading for Peking!

SHEN TE: The pilot can see us, let's wave!

They wave. The noise of the engine is louder.

MRS. YANG: You know that pilot up there?

SHEN TE: Wave, Mrs. Yang! I know the pilot who will be up there. He gave up hope. But he'll do it now. One man to raise himself above the misery, above us all. *(To the audience)*
Yang Sun, my lover:
Braving the storms
In company with the clouds
Crossing the heavens
And bringing to friends in faraway lands
The friendly mail!

In front of the inner curtain. Enter SHEN TE, *carrying* SHUI TA'S *mask. She sings.*

THE SONG OF THE DEFENSELESS

In our country
A useful man needs luck
Only if he finds strong backers
Can he prove himself useful.
The good can't defend themselves and
Even the gods are defenseless.

Oh, why don't the gods have their own ammunition
And launch against badness their own expedition
Enthroning the good and preventing sedition
And bringing the world to a peaceful condition?

Oh, why don't the gods do the buying and selling
Injustice forbidding, starvation dispelling
Give bread to each city and joy to each dwelling?
Oh, why don't the gods do the buying and selling?

She puts on SHUI TA'S *mask and sings in his voice.*

You can only help one of your luckless brothers
By trampling down a dozen others.
Why is it the gods do not feel indignation
And come down in fury to end exploitation
Defeat all defeat and forbid desperation
Refusing to tolerate such toleration?

Why is it?

5

Shen Te's tobacco shop. Behind the counter, MR. SHUI TA, *reading the paper.* MRS. SHIN *is cleaning up. She talks and he takes no notice.*

MRS. SHIN: And when certain rumors get about, what *happens* to a little place like this? It goes to pot. *I* know. So, if you want my advice, Mr. Shui Ta, find out just what has been going on between Miss Shen Te and that Yang Sun from Yellow Street. And remember: a certain interest in Miss Shen Te has been expressed by the barber next door, a man with twelve houses and only one wife, who, for that matter, is likely to drop off at any time. A certain interest has been expressed. He was even inquiring about her means and, if *that* doesn't prove a man is getting serious, what would? *(Still getting no response, she leaves with her bucket.)*

YANG SUN'S VOICE: Is that Miss Shen Te's tobacco shop?

MRS. SHIN'S VOICE: Yes, it is, but it's Mr. Shui Ta who's here today.

SHUI TA *runs to the mirror with the short, light steps of* SHEN TE, *and is just about to start primping, when he realizes his mistake, and turns away, with a short laugh. Enter* YANG SUN. MRS. SHIN *enters behind him and slips into the back room to eavesdrop.*

YANG SUN: I am Yang Sun. (SHUI TA *bows.*) Is Shen Te in?

SHUI TA: No.

YANG SUN: I guess you know our relationship? *(He is inspecting the stock.)* Quite a place! And I thought she was just talking big. I'll be flying again, all right. *(He takes a cigar, solicits and receives a light from* SHUI TA.*)* You think we can squeeze the other three hundred out of the tobacco stock?

SHUI TA: May I ask if it is your intention to sell at once?

YANG SUN: It was decent of her to come out with the two hundred but they aren't much use with the other three hundred still missing.

SHUI TA: Shen Te was overhasty promising so much. She might have to sell the shop itself to raise it. Haste, they say, is the wind that blows the house down.

YANG SUN: Oh, she isn't a girl to keep a man waiting. For one thing or the other, if you take my meaning.

SHUI TA: I take your meaning.

YANG SUN *(leering)*: Uh, huh.

SHUI TA: Would you explain what the five hundred silver dollars are for?

YANG SUN: Want to sound me out? Very well. The director of the Peking airfield is a friend of mine from flying school. I give him five hundred: he gets me the job.

SHUI TA: The price is high.

YANG SUN: Not as these things go. He'll have to fire one of the present pilots — for negligence. Only the man he has in mind isn't negligent. Not easy, you understand. You needn't mention that part of it to Shen Te.

SHUI TA *(looking intently at* YANG SUN): Mr. Yang Sun, you are asking my cousin to give up her possessions, leave her friends, and place her entire fate in your hands. I presume you intend to marry her?

YANG SUN: I'd be prepared to.

Slight pause.

SHUI TA: Those two hundred silver dollars would pay the rent here for six months. If you were Shen Te wouldn't you be tempted to continue in business?

YANG SUN: What? Can you imagine Yang Sun the flyer behind a counter? *(In an oily voice)* "A strong cigar or a mild one, worthy sir?" Not in this century!

SHUI TA: My cousin wishes to follow the promptings of her heart, and, from her own point of view, she may even have what is called the right to love. Accordingly, she has commissioned me to help you to this post. There is nothing here that I am not empowered to turn immediately into cash. Mrs. Mi Tzu, the landlady, will advise me about the sale.

Enter MRS. MI TZU.

MRS. MI TZU: Good morning, Mr. Shui Ta, you wish to see me about the rent? As you know it falls due the day after tomorrow.

SHUI TA: Circumstances have changed, Mrs. Mi Tzu: my cousin is getting married. Her future husband here, Mr. Yang Sun, will be taking her to Peking. I am interested in selling the tobacco stock.

MRS. MI TZU: How much are you asking, Mr. Shui Ta?

YANG SUN: Three hundred sil —

SHUI TA: Five hundred silver dollars.

MRS. MI TZU: How much did she pay for it, Mr. Shui Ta?

SHUI TA: A thousand. And very little has been sold.

MRS. MI TZU: She was robbed. But I'll make you a special offer if you'll promise to be out by the day after tomorrow. Three hundred silver dollars.

YANG SUN *(shrugging)*: Take it, man, take it.

SHUI TA: It is not enough.

YANG SUN: Why not? Why not? Certainly, it's enough.

SHUI TA: Five hundred silver dollars.

YANG SUN: But why? We only need three!

SHUI TA (*to* MRS. MI TZU): Excuse me. (*Takes* YANG SUN *on one side.*) The tobacco stock is pledged to the old couple who gave my cousin the two hundred.

YANG SUN: Is it in writing?

SHUI TA: No.

YANG SUN (*to* MRS. MI TZU): Three hundred will do.

MRS. MI TZU: Of course, I need an assurance that Miss Shen Te is not in debt.

YANG SUN: Mr. Shui Ta?

SHUI TA: She is not in debt.

YANG SUN: When can you let us have the money?

MRS. MI TZU: The day after tomorrow. And remember: I'm doing this because I have a soft spot in my heart for young lovers! (*Exit.*)

YANG SUN (*calling after her*): Boxes, jars, and sacks — three hundred for the lot and the pain's over! (*To* SHUI TA) Where else can we raise money by the day after tomorrow?

SHUI TA: Nowhere. Haven't you enough for the trip and the first few weeks?

YANG SUN: Oh, certainly.

SHUI TA: How much, exactly.

YANG SUN: Oh, I'll dig it up, even if I have to steal it.

SHUI TA: I see.

YANG SUN: Well, don't fall off the roof. I'll get to Peking somehow.

SHUI TA: Two people can't travel for nothing.

YANG SUN (*not giving* SHUI TA *a chance to answer*): I'm leaving *her* behind. No millstones round *my* neck!

SHUI TA: Oh.

YANG SUN: Don't look at me like that!

SHUI TA: How precisely is my cousin to live?

YANG SUN: Oh, you'll think of something.

SHUI TA: A small request, Mr. Yang Sun. Leave the two hundred silver dollars here until you can show me two tickets for Peking.

YANG SUN: You learn to mind your own business, Mr. Shui Ta.

SHUI TA: I'm afraid Miss Shen Te may not wish to sell the shop when she discovers that...

YANG SUN: You don't know women. She'll want to. Even then.

SHUI TA *(a slight outburst)*: She is a human being, sir! And not devoid of common sense!

YANG SUN: Shen Te is a woman: she *is* devoid of common sense. I only have to lay my hand on her shoulder, and church bells ring.

SHUI TA *(with difficulty)*: Mr. Yang Sun!

YANG SUN: Mr. Shui Whatever-it-is!

SHUI TA: My cousin is devoted to you... because...

YANG SUN: Because I have my hands on her breasts. Give me a cigar. *(He takes one for himself, stuffs a few more in his pocket, then changes his mind and takes the whole box.)* Tell her I'll marry her, then bring me the three hundred. Or let her bring it. One or the other. *(Exit.)*

MRS. SHIN *(sticking her head out of the back room)*: Well, he has your cousin under his thumb, and doesn't care if all Yellow Street knows it!

SHUI TA *(crying out)*: I've lost my shop! And he doesn't love me! *(He runs berserk through the room, repeating these lines incoherently. Then stops suddenly, and addresses* MRS. SHIN.*)* Mrs. Shin, you grew up in the gutter, like me. Are we lacking in hardness? I doubt it. If you steal a penny from me, I'll take you by the throat till you spit it out! You'd do the same to me. The times are bad, this city is hell, but we're like ants, we keep coming, up and up the walls, however smooth! Till bad luck comes. Being in love, for instance. One weakness is enough, and love is the deadliest.

MRS. SHIN *(emerging from the back room)*: You should have a little talk with Mr. Shu Fu, the barber. He's a real gentleman and just the thing for your cousin.
(She runs off.)

SHUI TA:

A caress becomes a stranglehold
A sigh of love turns to a cry of fear
Why are there vultures circling in the air?
A girl is going to meet her lover.

SHUI TA *sits down and* MR. SHU FU *enters with* MRS.
SHIN.

SHUI TA: Mr. Shu Fu?

SHU FU: Mr. Shui Ta.

They both bow.

SHUI TA: I am told that you have expressed a certain interest
in my cousin Shen Te. Let me set aside all propriety and
confess: she is at this moment in grave danger.

SHU FU: Oh dear!

SHUI TA: She has lost her shop, Mr. Shu Fu.

SHU FU: The charm of Miss Shen Te, Mr. Shui Ta, derives
from the goodness, not of her shop, but of her heart. Men
call her the Angel of the Slums.

SHUI TA: Yet her goodness has cost her two hundred silver
dollars in a single day; we must put a stop to it.

SHU FU: Permit me to differ, Mr. Shui Ta. Let us, rather, open
wide the gates to such goodness! Every morning, with pleasure
tinged by affection, I watch her charitable ministrations. For
they are hungry, and she giveth them to eat! Four of them,
to be precise. Why only four? I ask. Why not four hundred?
I hear she has been seeking shelter for the homeless. What
about my humble cabins behind the cattle run? They are at
her disposal. And so forth. And so on. Mr. Shui Ta, do you
think Miss Shen Te could be persuaded to listen to certain
ideas of mine? Ideas like these?

SHUI TA: Mr. Shu Fu, she would be honored.

Enter WONG *and the* POLICEMAN. MR. SHU FU *turns
abruptly away and studies the shelves.*

WONG: Is Miss Shen Te here?

SHUI TA: No.

WONG: I am Wong the water seller. You are Mr. Shui Ta?

SHUI TA: I am.

WONG: I am a friend of Shen Te's.

SHUI TA: An intimate friend, I hear.

WONG (*to the* POLICEMAN): You see? (*To* SHUI TA) It's because of my hand.

POLICEMAN: He hurt his hand, sir, that's a fact.

SHUI TA (*quickly*): You need a sling, I see. (*He takes a shawl from the back room, and throws it to* WONG.)

WONG: But that's her new shawl!

SHUI TA: She has no more use for it.

WONG: But she bought it to please someone!

SHUI TA: It happens to be no longer necessary.

WONG (*making the sling*): She is my only witness.

POLICEMAN: Mr. Shui Ta, your cousin is supposed to have seen the barber hit the water seller with a curling iron.

SHUI TA: I'm afraid my cousin was not present at the time.

WONG: But she was, sir! Just ask her! Isn't she in?

SHUI TA (*gravely*): Mr. Wong, my cousin has her own troubles. You wouldn't wish her to add to them by committing perjury?

WONG: But it was she that told me to go to the judge!

SHUI TA: Was the judge supposed to heal your hand?

MR. SHU FU *turns quickly around.* SHUI TA *bows to* MR. SHU FU, *and vice versa.*

WONG (*taking the sling off, and putting it back*): I see how it is.

POLICEMAN: Well, I'll be on my way. (*To* WONG) And you be careful. If Mr. Shu Fu wasn't a man who tempers justice with mercy, as the saying is, you'd be in jail for libel. Be off with you!

Exit WONG, *followed by* POLICEMAN.

SHUI TA: Profound apologies, Mr. Shu Fu.

SHUI FU: Not at all, Mr. Shui Ta. (*Pointing to the shawl*) The episode is over?

SHUI TA: It may take her time to recover. There are some fresh wounds.

SHU FU: We shall be discreet. Delicate. A short vacation could be arranged. . . .

SHUI TA: First of course, you and she would have to talk things over.

SHU FU: At a small supper in a small, but high-class, restaurant.

SHUI TA: I'll go and find her. *(Exit into back room.)*

MRS. SHIN *(sticking her head in again)*: Time for congratulations, Mr. Shu Fu?

SHU FU: Ah, Mrs. Shin! Please inform Miss Shen Te's guests they may take shelter in the cabins behind the cattle run!

MRS. SHIN *nods, grinning.*

SHU FU *(to the audience)*: Well? What do you think of me, ladies and gentlemen? What could a man do more? Could he be less selfish? More farsighted? A small supper in a small but . . . Does that bring rather vulgar and clumsy thoughts into your mind? Ts, ts, ts. Nothing of the sort will occur. She won't even be touched. Not even accidentally while passing the salt. An exchange of ideas only. Over the flowers on the table — white chrysanthemums, by the way *(he writes down a note of this)* — yes, over the white chrysanthemums, two young souls will . . . shall I say "find each other"? We shall NOT exploit the misfortunes of others. Understanding? Yes. An offer of assistance? Certainly. But quietly. Almost inaudibly. Perhaps with a single glance. A glance that could also — mean more.

MRS. SHIN *(coming forward)*: Everything under control, Mr. Shu Fu?

SHU FU: Oh, Mrs. Shin, what do you know about this worthless rascal Yang Sun?

MRS. SHIN: Why, he's the most worthless rascal . . .

SHU FU: Is he really? You're sure? *(As she opens her mouth)* From now on, he doesn't exist! Can't be found anywhere!

Enter YANG SUN.

YANG SUN: What's been going on here?

MRS. SHIN: Shall I call Mr. Shui Ta, Mr. Shu Fu? He wouldn't want strangers in here!

SHU FU: Mr. Shui Ta is in conference with Miss Shen Te. Not to be disturbed!

YANG SUN: Shen Te here? I didn't see her come in. What kind of conference?

SHU FU (*not letting him enter the back room*): Patience, dear sir! And if by chance I have an inkling who you are, pray take note that Miss Shen Te and I are about to announce our engagement.

YANG SUN: What?

MRS. SHIN: You didn't expect that, did you?

YANG SUN *is trying to push past the barber into the back room when* SHEN TE *comes out.*

SHU FU: My dear Shen Te, ten thousand apologies! Perhaps you . . .

YANG SUN: What is it, Shen Te? Have you gone crazy?

SHEN TE (*breathless*): My cousin and Mr. Shu Fu have come to an understanding. They wish me to hear Mr. Shu Fu's plans for helping the poor.

YANG SUN: Your cousin wants to part us.

SHEN TE: Yes.

YANG SUN: And you've agreed to it?

SHEN TE: Yes.

YANG SUN: They told you I was bad. (SHEN TE *is silent.*) And suppose I am. Does that make me need you less? I'm low, Shen Te, I have no money, I don't do the right thing but at least I put up a fight! (*He is near her now, and speaks in an undertone.*) Have you no eyes? Look at him. Have you forgotten already?

SHEN TE: No.

YANG SUN: How it was raining?

SHEN TE: No.

YANG SUN: How you cut me down from the willow tree? Bought me water? Promised me money to fly with?

SHEN TE *(shakily)*: Yang Sun, what do you want?

YANG SUN: I want you to come with me.

SHEN TE *(in a small voice)*: Forgive me, Mr. Shu Fu, I want to go with Mr. Yang Sun.

YANG SUN: We're lovers you know. Give me the key to the shop. (SHEN TE *takes the key from around her neck.* YANG SUN *puts it on the counter. To* MRS. SHIN) Leave it under the mat when you're through. Let's go, Shen Te.

SHU FU: But this is rape! Mr. Shui Ta!!

YANG SUN *(to* SHEN TE): Tell him not to shout.

SHEN TE: Please don't shout for my cousin, Mr. Shu Fu. He doesn't agree with me, I know, but he's wrong. *(To the audience)*

> I want to go with the man I love
> I don't want to count the cost
> I don't want to consider if it's wise
> I don't want to know if he loves me
> I want to go with the man I love.

YANG SUN: That's the spirit.

And the couple leave.

In front of the inner curtain. SHEN TE *in her wedding clothes, on the way to her wedding.*

SHEN TE: Something terrible has happened. As I left the shop with Yang Sun, I found the old carpet dealer's wife waiting on the street, trembling all over. She told me her husband had taken to his bed — sick with all the worry and excitement over the two hundred silver dollars they lent me. She said it would be best if I gave it back now. Of course, I had to say I would. She said she couldn't quite trust my cousin Shui Ta or even my fiancé Yang Sun. There were tears in her eyes. With my emotions in an uproar, I threw myself into Yang Sun's arms, I couldn't resist him. The things he'd said to Shui Ta had taught Shen Te nothing. Sinking into his arms, I said to myself:
    To let no one perish, not even oneself
    To fill everyone with happiness, even oneself
    Is so good

How could I have forgotten those two old people? Yang Sun swept me away like a small hurricane. But he's not a bad man, and he loves me. He'd rather work in the cement factory than owe his flying to a crime. Though, of course, flying *is* a great passion with Sun. Now, on the way to my wedding, I waver between fear and joy.

6

The "private dining room" on the upper floor of a cheap restau-
rant in a poor section of town. With SHEN TE: *the* GRANDFA-
THER, *the* SISTER-IN-LAW, *the* NIECE, MRS. SHIN, *the* UN-
EMPLOYED MAN. *In a corner, alone, a* PRIEST. *A* WAITER
pouring wine. Downstage, YANG SUN *talking to his* MOTHER.
He wears a dinner jacket.

YANG SUN: Bad news, Mamma. She came right out and told
me she can't sell the shop for me. Some idiot is bringing a
claim because he lent her the two hundred she gave you.

MRS. YANG: What did you say? Of course, you can't marry
her now.

YANG SUN: It's no use saying anything to *her.* I've sent for her
cousin, Mr. Shui Ta. He said there was nothing in writing.

MRS. YANG: Good idea. I'll go out and look for him. Keep an
eye on things.

Exit MRS. YANG. SHEN TE *has been pouring wine.*

SHEN TE *(to the audience, pitcher in hand)*: I wasn't mistaken
in him. He's bearing up well. Though it must have been an

awful blow — giving up flying. I do love him so. *(Calling across the room to him)* Sun, you haven't drunk a toast with the bride!

YANG SUN: What do we drink to?

SHEN TE: Why, to the future!

YANG SUN: When the bridegroom's dinner jacket won't be a hired one!

SHEN TE: But when the bride's dress will still get rained on sometimes!

YANG SUN: To everything we ever wished for!

SHEN TE: May all our dreams come true!

They drink.

YANG SUN *(with loud conviviality)*: And now, friends, before the wedding gets under way, I have to ask the bride a few questions. I've no idea what kind of a wife she'll make, and it worries me. *(Wheeling on* SHEN TE*)* For example. Can you make five cups of tea with three tea leaves?

SHEN TE: No.

YANG SUN: So I won't be getting very much tea. Can you sleep on a straw mattress the size of that book? *(He points to the large volume the* PRIEST *is reading.)*

SHEN TE: The two of us?

YANG SUN: The one of you.

SHEN TE: In that case, no.

YANG SUN: What a wife! I'm shocked!

While the audience is laughing, his MOTHER *returns. With a shrug of her shoulders, she tells* SUN *the expected guest hasn't arrived. The* PRIEST *shuts the book with a bang, and makes for the door.*

MRS. YANG: Where are *you* off to? It's only a matter of minutes.

PRIEST *(watch in hand)*: Time goes on, Mrs. Yang, and I've another wedding to attend to. Also a funeral.

MRS. YANG *(irately)*: D'you think we planned it this way? I was hoping to manage with one pitcher of wine, and we've run through two already. *(Points to empty pitcher. Loudly)* My dear Shen Te, I don't know where your cousin can be keeping himself!

SHEN TE: My cousin?!

MRS. YANG: Certainly. I'm old-fashioned enough to think such a close relative should attend the wedding.

SHEN TE: Oh, Sun, is it the three hundred silver dollars?

YANG SUN *(not looking her in the eye)*: Are you deaf? Mother says she's old-fashioned. And I say I'm considerate. We'll wait another fifteen minutes.

HUSBAND: Another fifteen minutes.

MRS. YANG *(addressing the company)*: Now you all know, don't you, that my son is getting a job as a mail pilot?

SISTER-IN-LAW: In Peking, too, isn't it?

MRS. YANG: In Peking, too! The two of us are moving to Peking!

SHEN TE: Sun, tell your mother Peking is out of the question now.

YANG SUN: Your cousin'll tell her. If he agrees. I don't agree.

SHEN TE *(amazed, and dismayed)*: Sun!

YANG SUN: I hate this godforsaken Setzuan. What people! Know what they look like when I half close my eyes? Horses! Whinnying, fretting, stamping, screwing their necks up! *(Loudly)* And what is it the thunder says? They are su-per-flu-ous! *(He hammers out the syllables.)* They've run their last race! They can go trample themselves to death! *(Pause.)* I've got to get out of here.

SHEN TE: But I've promised the money to the old couple.

YANG SUN: And since you always do the wrong thing, it's lucky your cousin's coming. Have another drink.

SHEN TE *(quietly)*: My cousin can't be coming.

YANG SUN: How d'you mean?

SHEN TE: My cousin can't be where I am.

YANG SUN: Quite a conundrum!

SHEN TE *(desperately)*: Sun, I'm the one that loves you. Not my cousin. He was thinking of the job in Peking when he promised you the old couple's money—

YANG SUN: Right. And that's why he's bringing the three hundred silver dollars. Here — to my wedding.

SHEN TE: He is not bringing the three hundred silver dollars.

YANG SUN: Huh? What makes you think that?

SHEN TE *(looking into his eyes)*: He says you only bought one ticket to Peking.

Short pause.

YANG SUN: That was yesterday. *(He pulls two tickets part way out of his inside pocket, making her look under his coat.)* Two tickets. I don't want Mother to know. She'll get left behind. I sold her furniture to buy these tickets, so you see . . .

SHEN TE: But what's to become of the old couple?

YANG SUN: What's to become of me? Have another drink. Or do you believe in moderation? If I drink, I fly again. And if you drink, you may learn to understand me.

SHEN TE: You want to fly. But I can't help you.

YANG SUN: "Here's a plane, my darling — but it's only got one wing!"

The WAITER enters.

WAITER: Mrs. Yang!

MRS. YANG: Yes?

WAITER: Another pitcher of wine, ma'am?

MRS. YANG: We have enough, thanks. Drinking makes me sweat.

WAITER: Would you mind paying, ma'am?

MRS. YANG *(to everyone)*: Just be patient a few moments longer, everyone, Mr. Shui Ta is on his way over! *(To the WAITER)* Don't be a spoilsport.

WAITER: I can't let you leave till you've paid your bill, ma'am.

MRS. YANG: But they know me here!

WAITER: That's just it.

PRIEST *(ponderously getting up)*: I humbly take my leave. *(And he does.)*

MRS. YANG *(to the others, desperately)*: Stay where you are, everybody! The priest says he'll be back in two minutes!

YANG SUN: It's no good, Mamma. Ladies and gentlemen, Mr. Shui Ta still hasn't arrived and the priest has gone home. We won't detain you any longer.

They are leaving now.

GRANDFATHER *(in the doorway, having forgotten to put his glass down)*: To the bride! *(He drinks, puts down the glass, and follows the others.)*

Pause.

SHEN TE: Shall I go too?

YANG SUN: You? Aren't you the bride? Isn't this your wedding? *(He drags her across the room, tearing her wedding dress.)* If we can wait, you can wait. Mother calls me her falcon. She wants to see me in the clouds. But I think it may be St. Nevercome's Day before she'll go to the door and see my plane thunder by. *(Pause. He pretends the guests are still present.)* Why such a lull in the conversation, ladies and gentlemen? Don't you like it here? The ceremony is only slightly postponed—because an important guest is expected at any moment. Also because the bride doesn't know what love is. While we're waiting, the bridegroom will sing a little song. *(He does so.)*

THE SONG OF ST. NEVERCOME'S DAY

On a certain day, as is generally known,
    One and all will be shouting: Hooray, hooray!
For the beggar maid's son has a solid-gold throne
    And the day is St. Nevercome's Day
On St. Nevercome's, Nevercome's, Nevercome's Day
    He'll sit on his solid-gold throne

Oh, hooray, hooray! That day goodness will pay!
    That day badness will cost you your head!
And merit and money will smile and be funny
    While exchanging salt and bread

On St. Nevercome's, Nevercome's, Nevercome's Day
   While exchanging salt and bread

And the grass, oh, the grass will look down at the sky
   And the pebbles will roll up the stream
And all men will be good without batting an eye
   They will make of our earth a dream
On St. Nevercome's, Nevercome's, Nevercome's Day
   They will make of our earth a dream

And as for me, that's the day I shall be
   A flyer and one of the best
Unemployed man, you will have work to do
   Washerwoman, you'll get your rest
On St. Nevercome's, Nevercome's, Nevercome's Day
   Washerwoman, you'll get your rest

MRS. YANG: It looks like he's not coming.
The three of them sit looking at the door.

Wong's den. The sewer pipe is again transparent and again the
GODS *appear to* WONG *in a dream.*

WONG: I'm so glad you've come, illustrious ones. It's Shen Te.
  She's in great trouble from following the rule about loving
  thy neighbor. Perhaps she's *too* good for this world!
FIRST GOD: Nonsense! You are eaten up by lice and doubts!
WONG: Forgive me, illustrious one, I only meant you might
  deign to intervene.
FIRST GOD: Out of the question! My colleague here inter-
  vened in some squabble or other only yesterday. *(He points
  to the* THIRD GOD *who has a black eye.)* The results are be-
  fore us!
WONG: She had to call on her cousin again. But not even he
  could help. I'm afraid the shop is done for.
THIRD GOD *(a little concerned)*: Perhaps we should help after
  all?
FIRST GOD: The gods help those that help themselves.
WONG: What if we *can't* help ourselves, illustrious ones?

Slight pause.

SECOND GOD: Try, anyway! Suffering ennobles!

FIRST GOD: Our faith in Shen Te is unshaken!

THIRD GOD: We certainly haven't found any *other* good people. You can see where we spend our nights from the straw
on our clothes.

WONG: You might help her find her way by —

FIRST GOD: The good man finds his own way here below!

SECOND GOD: The good woman too.

FIRST GOD: The heavier the burden, the greater her strength!

THIRD GOD: We're only onlookers, you know.

FIRST GOD: And everything will be all right in the end, O ye
of little faith!

They are gradually disappearing through these last lines.

7

The yard behind Shen Te's shop. A few articles of furniture on a cart.
SHEN TE *and* MRS. SHIN *are taking the washing off the line.*

MRS. SHIN: If you ask me, you should fight tooth and nail to keep the shop.
SHEN TE: How can I? I have to sell the tobacco to pay back the two hundred silver dollars today.
MRS. SHIN: No husband, no tobacco, no house and home! What are you going to live on?
SHEN TE: I can work. I can sort tobacco.
MRS. SHIN: Hey, look, Mr. Shui Ta's trousers! He must have left here stark naked!
SHEN TE: Oh, he may have another pair, Mrs. Shin.
MRS. SHIN: But if he's gone for good as you say, why has he left his pants behind?
SHEN TE: Maybe he's thrown them away.
MRS. SHIN: Can I take them?
SHEN TE: Oh, no.
    Enter MR. SHU FU, *running.*

SHU FU: Not a word! Total silence! I know all. You have sacrificed your own love and happiness so as not to hurt a dear old couple who had put their trust in you! Not in vain does this district—for all its malevolent tongues—call you the Angel of the Slums! That young man couldn't rise to your level, so you left him. And now, when I see you closing up the little shop, that veritable haven of rest for the multitude, well, I cannot, I cannot let it pass. Morning after morning I have stood watching in the doorway not unmoved—while you graciously handed out rice to the wretched. Is that never to happen again? Is the good woman of Setzuan to disappear? If only you would allow *me* to assist you! Now don't say anything! No assurances, no exclamations of gratitude! *(He has taken out his checkbook.)* Here! A blank check. *(He places it on the cart.)* Just my signature. Fill it out as you wish. Any sum in the world. I herewith retire from the scene, quietly, unobtrusively, making no claims, on tiptoe, full of veneration, absolutely selflessly...

(He has gone.)

MRS. SHIN: Well! You're saved. There's always some idiot of a man.... Now hurry! Put down a thousand silver dollars and let me fly to the bank before he comes to his senses.

SHEN TE: I can pay you for the washing without any check.

MRS. SHIN: What? You're not going to cash it just because you might have to marry him? Are you crazy? Men like him *want* to be led by the nose! Are you still thinking of that flyer? All Yellow Street knows how he treated you!

SHEN TE:

When I heard his cunning laugh, I was afraid
But when I saw the holes in his shoes, I loved him dearly.

MRS. SHIN: Defending that good-for-nothing after all that's happened!

SHEN TE *(staggering as she holds some of the washing)*: Oh!

MRS. SHIN *(taking the washing from her, dryly)*: So you feel dizzy when you stretch and bend? There couldn't be a little visitor on the way? If that's it, you can forget Mr. Shu Fu's blank check: it wasn't meant for a christening present!

She goes to the back with a basket. SHEN TE'S *eyes follow* MRS. SHIN *for a moment. Then she looks down at her own body, feels her stomach, and a great joy comes into her eyes.*

SHEN TE: O joy! A new human being is on the way. The world awaits him. In the cities the people say: he's got to be reckoned with, this new human being! *(She imagines a little boy to be present, and introduces him to the audience.)* This is my son, the well-known flyer!

Say: Welcome

To the conqueror of unknown mountains and unreachable regions

Who brings us our mail across the impassable deserts!

She leads him up and down by the hand.

Take a look at the world, my son. That's a tree. Tree, yes. Say: "Hello, tree!" And bow. Like this. *(She bows.)* Now you know each other. And, look, here comes the water seller. He's a friend, give him your hand. A cup of fresh water for my little son, please. Yes, it *is* a warm day. *(Handing the cup.)* Oh dear, a policeman, we'll have to make a circle round *him.* Perhaps we can pick a few cherries over there in the rich Mr. Pung's garden. But we mustn't be seen. You want cherries? Just like children with fathers. No, no, you can't go straight at them like that. Don't pull. We must learn to be reasonable. Well, have it your own way. *(She has let him make for the cherries.)* Can you reach? Where to put them? Your mouth is the best place. *(She tries one herself.)* Mmm, they're good. But the policeman, we must run! *(They run.)* Yes, back to the street. Calm now, so no one will notice us. *(Walking the street with her child, she sings.)*

Once a plum — 'twas in Japan —

Made a conquest of a man

But the man's turn soon did come

For he gobbled up the plum

Enter WONG, *with a* CHILD *by the hand. He coughs.*

SHEN TE: Wong!

WONG: It's about the carpenter, Shen Te. He's lost his shop, and he's been drinking. His children are on the streets. This is one. Can you help?

SHEN TE (*to the* CHILD): Come here, little man. (*Takes him down to the footlights. To the audience*)

You there! A man is asking you for shelter!

A man of tomorrow says: what about today?

His friend the conqueror, whom you know,

Is his advocate!

(*To* WONG) He can live in Mr. Shu Fu's cabins. I may have to go there myself. I'm going to have a baby. That's a secret — don't tell Yang Sun — we'd only be in his way. Can you find the carpenter for me?

WONG: I knew you'd think of something. (*To the* CHILD) Good-bye son, I'm going for your father.

SHEN TE: What about your hand, Wong? I wanted to help, but my cousin . . .

WONG: Oh, I can get along with one hand, don't worry.

(*He shows how he can handle his pole with his left hand alone.*)

SHEN TE: But your right hand! Look, take this cart, sell everything that's on it, and go to the doctor with the money . . .

WONG: She's still good. But first I'll bring the carpenter. I'll pick up the cart when I get back. (*Exit* WONG.)

SHEN TE (*to the* CHILD): Sit down over here, son, till your father comes.

The CHILD *sits crosslegged on the ground. Enter the* HUSBAND *and* WIFE, *each dragging a large, full sack.*

WIFE (*furtively*): You're alone, Shen Te, dear?

SHEN TE *nods. The* WIFE *beckons to the nephew offstage. He comes on with another sack.*

WIFE: Your cousin's away? (SHEN TE *nods.*) He's not coming back?

SHEN TE: No. I'm giving up the shop.

WIFE: That's why we're here. We want to know if we can leave these things in your new home. Will you do us this favor?

SHEN TE: Why, yes, I'd be glad to.

HUSBAND *(cryptically)*: And if anyone asks about them, say they're yours.

SHEN TE: Would anyone ask?

WIFE *(with a glance back at her husband)*: Oh, someone might. The police, for instance. They don't seem to like us. Where can we put it?

SHEN TE: Well, I'd rather not get in any more trouble...

WIFE: Listen to her! The good woman of Setzuan!

SHEN TE *is silent.*

HUSBAND: There's enough tobacco in those sacks to give us a new start in life. We could have our own tobacco factory!

SHEN TE *(slowly)*: You'll have to put them in the back room.

The sacks are taken offstage, while the CHILD *is alone. Shyly glancing around him, he goes to the garbage can, starts playing with the contents, and eating some of the scraps. The others return.*

WIFE: We're counting on you, Shen Te!

SHEN TE: Yes. *(She sees the* CHILD *and is shocked.)*

HUSBAND: We'll see you in Mr. Shu Fu's cabins.

NEPHEW: The day after tomorrow.

SHEN TE: Yes. Now go. Go! I'm not feeling well.

Exeunt all three, virtually pushed off.

He is eating the refuse in the garbage can!

Only look at his little gray mouth!

Pause. Music.

As this is the world *my* son will enter
I will study to defend him.
To be good to you, my son,
I shall be a tigress to all others
If I have to.
And I shall have to.

She starts to go.

One more time, then. I hope really the last.

Exit SHEN TE, *taking Shui Ta's trousers.* MRS. SHIN *enters and watches her with marked interest. Enter the* SISTER-IN-LAW *and the* GRANDFATHER.

SISTER-IN-LAW: So it's true, the shop has closed down. And the furniture's in the back yard. It's the end of the road!

MRS. SHIN (*pompously*): The fruit of high living, selfishness, and sensuality! Down the primrose path to Mr. Shu Fu's cabins—with you!

SISTER-IN-LAW: Cabins? Rat holes! He gave them to us because his soap supplies only went moldy there!

Enter the UNEMPLOYED MAN.

UNEMPLOYED MAN: Shen Te is moving?

SISTER-IN-LAW: Yes. She was sneaking away.

MRS. SHIN: She's ashamed of herself, and no wonder!

UNEMPLOYED MAN: Tell her to call Mr. Shui Ta or she's done for this time!

SISTER-IN-LAW: Tell her to call Mr. Shui Ta or *we're* done for this time!

Enter WONG *and* CARPENTER, *the latter with a* CHILD *on each hand.*

CARPENTER: So we'll have a roof over our heads for a change!

MRS. SHIN: Roof? Whose roof?

CARPENTER: Mr. Shu Fu's cabins. And we have little Feng to thank for it. (*Feng, we find, is the name of the* CHILD *already there; his* FATHER *now takes him. To the other* TWO) Bow to your little brother, you two!

The CARPENTER *and the* TWO NEW ARRIVALS *bow to* FENG.

Enter SHUI TA.

UNEMPLOYED MAN: Sst! Mr. Shui Ta!

Pause.

SHUI TA: And what is this crowd here for, may I ask?

WONG: How do you do, Mr. Shui Ta. This is the carpenter. Miss Shen Te promised him space in Mr. Shu Fu's cabins.

SHUI TA: That will not be possible.

CARPENTER: We can't go there after all?

SHUI TA: All the space is needed for other purposes.

SISTER-IN-LAW: You mean we have to get out? But we've got nowhere to go.

SHUI TA: Miss Shen Te finds it possible to provide employment. If the proposition interests you, you may stay in the cabins.

SISTER-IN-LAW *(with distaste)*: You mean *work*? Work for Miss Shen Te?

SHUI TA: Making tobacco, yes. There are three bales here already. Would you like to get them?

SISTER-IN-LAW *(trying to bluster)*: We have our own tobacco! We were in the tobacco business before you were born!

SHUI TA *(to the* CARPENTER *and the* UNEMPLOYED MAN*)*: You *don't* have your own tobacco. What about you?

The CARPENTER *and the* UNEMPLOYED MAN *get the point, and go for the sacks. Enter* MRS. MI TZU.

MRS. MI TZU: Mr. Shui Ta? I've brought you your three hundred silver dollars.

SHUI TA: I'll sign your lease instead. I've decided not to sell.

MRS. MI TZU: What? You don't need the money for that flyer?

SHUI TA: No.

MRS. MI TZU: And you can pay six months' rent?

SHUI TA *(takes the barber's blank check from her cart and fills it out)*: Here is a check for ten thousand silver dollars. On Mr. Shu Fu's account. Look! *(He shows her the signature on the check.)* Your six months' rent will be in your hands by seven this evening. And now, if you'll excuse me.

MRS. MI TZU: So it's Mr. Shu Fu now. The flyer has been given his walking papers. These modern girls! In my day they'd have said she was flighty. That poor, deserted Mr. Yang Sun! *Exit* MRS. MI TZU. *The* CARPENTER *and the* UNEMPLOYED MAN *drag the three sacks back on the stage.*

CARPENTER (*to* SHUI TA): I don't know why I'm doing this for you.

SHUI TA: Perhaps your children want to eat, Mr. Carpenter.

SISTER-IN-LAW (*catching sight of the sacks*): Was my brother-in-law here?

MRS. SHIN: Yes, he was.

SISTER-IN-LAW: I thought as much. I know those sacks! That's our tobacco!

SHUI TA: Really? I thought it came from my back room! Shall we consult the police on the point?

SISTER-IN-LAW (*defeated*): No.

SHUI TA: Perhaps you will show me the way to Mr. Shu Fu's cabins? *Taking* FENG *by the hand,* SHUI TA *goes off, followed by the* CARPENTER *and his* TWO OLDER CHILDREN, *the* SISTER-IN-LAW, *the* GRANDFATHER, *and the* UNEMPLOYED MAN. *Each of the last three drags a sack. Enter* OLD MAN *and* OLD WOMAN.

MRS. SHIN: A pair of pants — missing from the clothes line one minute — and next minute on the honorable backside of Mr. Shui Ta.

OLD WOMAN: We thought Miss Shen Te was here.

MRS. SHIN (*preoccupied*): Well, she's not.

OLD MAN: There was something she was going to give us.

WONG: She was going to help me too. (*Looking at his hand*) It'll be too late soon. But she'll be back. This cousin has never stayed long.

MRS. SHIN (*approaching a conclusion*): No, he hasn't, has he?

The Sewer Pipe: WONG *asleep. In his dream, he tells the* GODS *his fears. The* GODS *seem tired from all their travels. They stop for a moment and look over their shoulders at the water seller.*

WONG: Illustrious ones. I've been having a bad dream. Our beloved Shen Te was in great distress in the rushes down by the river — the spot where the bodies of suicides are washed up. She kept staggering and holding her head down as if she was carrying something and it was dragging her down into the mud. When I called out to her, she said she had to take your Book of Rules to the other side, and not get it wet, or the ink would come off. You had talked to her about the virtues, you know, the time she gave you shelter in Setzuan.

THIRD GOD: Well, but what do you suggest, my dear Wong?

WONG: Maybe a little relaxation of the rules, Benevolent One, in view of the bad times.

THIRD GOD: As for instance?

WONG: Well, um, good-will, for instance, might do instead of love?

THIRD GOD: I'm afraid that would create new problems.

WONG: Or, instead of justice, good sportsmanship?

THIRD GOD: That would only mean more work.

WONG: Instead of honor, outward propriety?

THIRD GOD: Still more work! No, no! The rules will have to stand, my dear Wong!

Wearily shaking their heads, all three journey on.

8

Shui Ta's tobacco factory in Shu Fu's cabins. Huddled together be-hind bars, several FAMILIES, *mostly women and children. Among these people the* SISTER-IN-LAW, *the* GRANDFATHER, *the* CAR-PENTER, *and his* THREE CHILDREN. *Enter* MRS. YANG *fol-lowed by* YANG SUN.

MRS. YANG *(to the audience)*: There's something I just *have* to tell you: strength and wisdom are wonderful things. The strong and wise Mr. Shui Ta has transformed my son from a dissipated good-for-nothing into a model citizen. As you may have heard, Mr. Shui Ta opened a small tobacco factory near the cattle runs. It flourished. Three months ago — I shall nev-er forget it — I asked for an appointment and Mr. Shui Ta agreed to see us — me and my son. I can see him now as he came through the door to meet us. . . .
Enter SHUI TA, *from a door.*
SHUI TA: What can I do for you, Mrs. Yang?
MRS. YANG: This morning the police came to the house. We find you've brought an action for breach of promise of mar-

riage. In the name of Shen Te. You also claim that Sun came by two hundred silver dollars by improper means.

SHUI TA: That is correct.

MRS. YANG: Mr. Shui Ta, the money's all gone. When the Peking job didn't materialize, he ran through it all in three days. I know he's a good-for-nothing. He sold my furniture. He was moving to Peking without me. Miss Shen Te thought highly of him at one time.

SHUI TA: What do *you* say, Mr. Yang Sun?

YANG SUN: The money's gone.

SHUI TA (*to* MRS. YANG): Mrs. Yang, in consideration of my cousin's incomprehensible weakness for your son, I am prepared to give him another chance. He can have a job — here. The two hundred silver dollars will be taken out of his wages.

YANG SUN: So it's the factory or jail?

SHUI TA: Take your choice.

YANG SUN: May I speak with Shen Te?

SHUI TA: You may not.

Pause.

YANG SUN (*sullenly*): Show me where to go.

MRS. YANG: Mr. Shui Ta, you are kindness itself: the gods will reward you! (*To* YANG SUN) And honest work will make a man of you, my boy. (YANG SUN *follows* SHUI TA *into the factory.* MRS. YANG *comes down again to the footlights.*) Actually, honest work didn't agree with him — at first. And he got no opportunity to distinguish himself till — in the third week — when the wages were being paid . . .

SHUI TA *has a bag of money. Standing next to his foreman — the former* UNEMPLOYED MAN — *he counts out the wages. It is* YANG SUN'S *turn.*

UNEMPLOYED MAN (*reading*): Carpenter, six silver dollars. Yang Sun, six silver dollars.

YANG SUN (*quietly*): Excuse me, sir. I don't think it can be more than five. May I see? (*He takes the foreman's list.*) It says six working days. But that's a mistake, sir. I took a day off for court business. And I won't take what I haven't earned, however miserable the pay is!

UNEMPLOYED MAN: Yang Sun. Five silver dollars. (*To* SHUI TA) A rare case, Mr. Shui Ta!

SHUI TA: How is it the books says six when it should say five?

UNEMPLOYED MAN: I must've made a mistake, Mr. Shui Ta. (*With a look at* YANG SUN) It won't happen again.

SHUI TA (*taking* YANG SUN *aside*): You don't hold back, do you? You give your all to the firm. You're even honest. Do the foreman's mistakes always favor the workers?

YANG SUN: He does have . . . friends.

SHUI TA: Thank you. May I offer you any little recompense?

YANG SUN: Give me a trial period of one week, and I'll prove my intelligence is worth more to you than my strength.

MRS. YANG (*still down at the footlights*): Fighting words, fighting words! That evening, I said to Sun: "If you're a flyer, then fly, my falcon! Rise in the world!" And he got to be foreman. Yes, in Mr. Shui Ta's tobacco factory, he worked real miracles.

We see YANG SUN *with his legs apart standing behind the* WORKERS *who are handing along a basket of raw tobacco above their heads.*

YANG SUN: Faster! Faster! You, there, d'you think you can just stand around, now you're not foreman any more? It'll be your job to lead us in song. Sing!

UNEMPLOYED MAN *starts singing. The others join in the refrain.*

SONG OF THE EIGHTH ELEPHANT

Chang had seven elephants — all much the same —
    But then there was Little Brother
The seven, they were wild, Little Brother, he was tame
    And to guard them Chang chose Little Brother

Run faster!
Mr. Chang has a forest park
Which must be cleared before tonight
And already it's growing dark!

When the seven elephants cleared that forest park
  Mr. Chang rode high on Little Brother
While the seven toiled and moiled till dark
  On his big behind sat Little Brother
    Dig faster!
    Mr. Chang has a forest park
    Which must be cleared before tonight
    And already it's growing dark!

And the seven elephants worked many an hour
  Till none of them could work another
Old Chang, he looked sour, on the seven he did glower
  But gave a pound of rice to Little Brother
    What was that?
    Mr. Chang has a forest park
    Which must be cleared before tonight.
    And already it's growing dark!

And the seven elephants hadn't any tusks
  The one that had the tusks was Little Brother
Seven are no match for one, if the one has a gun!
  How old Chang did laugh at Little Brother!
    Keep on digging!
    Mr. Chang has a forest park
    Which must be cleared before tonight
    And already it's growing dark!

Smoking a cigar, SHUI TA *strolls by.* YANG SUN, *laughing, has joined in the refrain of the third stanza and speeded up the tempo of the last stanza by clapping his hands.*

MRS. YANG: And that's why I say: strength and wisdom are wonderful things. It took the strong and wise Mr. Shui Ta to bring out the best in Yang Sun. A real superior man is like a bell. If you ring it, it rings, and if you don't, it don't, as the saying is.

9

Shen Te's shop, now an office with club chairs and fine carpets. It is raining. SHUI TA, *now fat, is just dismissing the* OLD MAN *and* OLD WOMAN. MRS. SHIN, *in obviously new clothes, looks on, smirking.*

SHUI TA: No! I cannot tell you when we expect her back.

OLD WOMAN: The two hundred silver dollars came today. In an envelope. There was no letter, but it must be from Shen Te. We want to write and thank her. May we have her address?

SHUI TA: I'm afraid I haven't got it.

OLD MAN (*pulling* OLD WOMAN'S *sleeve*): Let's be going.

OLD WOMAN: She's got to come back sometime!

They move off, uncertainly, worried. SHUI TA *bows.*

MRS. SHIN: They lost the carpet shop because they couldn't pay their taxes. The money arrived too late.

SHUI TA: They could have come to me.

MRS. SHIN: People don't like coming to you.

SHUI TA (*sits suddenly, one hand to his head*): I'm dizzy.

MRS. SHIN: After all, you *are* in your seventh month. But old Mrs. Shin will be there in your hour of trial! *(She cackles feebly.)*

SHUI TA *(in a stifled voice)*: Can I count on that?

MRS. SHIN: We all have our price, and mine won't be too high for the great Mr. Shui Ta! *(She opens* SHUI TA'S *collar.)*

SHUI TA: It's for the child's sake. All of this.

MRS. SHIN: "All for the child," of course.

SHUI TA: I'm so fat. People must notice.

MRS. SHIN: Oh no, they think it's 'cause you're rich.

SHUI TA *(more feelingly)*: What will happen to the child?

MRS. SHIN: You ask that nine times a day. Why, it'll have the best that money can buy!

SHUI TA: He must never see Shui Ta.

MRS. SHIN: Oh, no. Always Shen Te.

SHUI TA: What about the neighbors? There are rumors, aren't there?

MRS. SHIN: As long as Mr. Shu Fu doesn't find out, there's nothing to worry about. Drink this.

Enter YANG SUN *in a smart business suit, and carrying a businessman's briefcase.* SHUI TA *is more or less in* MRS. SHIN'S *arms.*

YANG SUN *(surprised)*: I guess I'm in the way.

SHUI TA *(ignoring this, rises with an effort)*: Till tomorrow, Mrs. Shin.

MRS. SHIN *leaves with a smile, putting her new gloves on.*

YANG SUN: Gloves now! She couldn't be fleecing you? And since when did *you* have a private life? *(Taking a paper from the briefcase)* You haven't been at your best lately, and things are getting out of hand. The police want to close us down. They say that at the most they can only permit twice the lawful number of workers.

SHUI TA *(evasively)*: The cabins are quite good enough.

YANG SUN: For the workers maybe, not for the tobacco. They're too damp. We must take over some of Mrs. Mi Tzu's buildings.

SHUI TA: Her price is double what I can pay.

YANG SUN: Not unconditionally. If she has me to stroke her knees she'll come down.

SHUI TA: I'll never agree to that.

YANG SUN: What's wrong? Is it the rain? You get so irritable whenever it rains.

SHUI TA: Never! I will never...

YANG SUN: Mrs. Mi Tzu'll be here in five minutes. *You* fix it. And Shu Fu will be with her.... What's all that noise?

During the above dialogue, WONG *is heard offstage, calling* "The good Shen Te, where is she? Which of you has seen Shen Te, good people? Where is Shen Te?" *A knock. Enter* WONG.

WONG: Mr. Shui Ta, I've come to ask when Miss Shen Te will be back, it's six months now.... There are rumors. People say something's happened to her.

SHUI TA: I'm busy. Come back next week.

WONG *(excited)*: In the morning there was always rice on her doorstep — for the needy. It's been there again lately!

SHUI TA: And what do people conclude from this?

WONG: That Shen Te is still in Setzuan! She's been... *(He breaks off.)*

SHUI TA: She's been what? Mr. Wong, if you're Shen Te's friend, talk a little less about her, that's my advice to you.

WONG: I don't want your advice! Before she disappeared, Miss Shen Te told me something very important — she's pregnant!

YANG SUN: What? What was that?

SHUI TA *(quickly)*: The man is lying.

WONG: A good woman isn't so easily forgotten, Mr. Shui Ta.

He leaves. SHUI TA *goes quickly into the back room.*

YANG SUN *(to the audience)*: Shen Te pregnant? So that's why. Her cousin sent her away, so I wouldn't get wind of it. I have a son, a Yang appears on the scene, and what happens? Mother and child vanish into thin air! That scoundrel, that unspeakable . . . *(The sound of sobbing is heard from the back room.)* What was that? Someone sobbing? Who was it? Mr. Shui Ta the Tobacco King doesn't weep his heart out. And where does the rice come from that's on the doorstep in the morning? (SHUI TA *returns. He goes to the door and looks out into the rain.)* Where is she?

SHUI TA: Sh! It's nine o'clock. But the rain's so heavy, you can't hear a thing.

YANG SUN: What do you want to hear?

SHUI TA: The mail plane.

YANG SUN: What?!

SHUI TA: I've been told *you* wanted to fly at one time. Is that all forgotten?

YANG SUN: Flying mail is night work. I prefer the daytime. And the firm is very dear to me — after all it belongs to my ex-fiancée, even if she's not around. And she's not, is she?

SHUI TA: What do you mean by that?

YANG SUN: Oh, well, let's say I haven't altogether — lost interest.

SHUI TA: My cousin might like to know that.

YANG SUN: I might not be indifferent — if I found she was being kept under lock and key.

SHUI TA: By whom?

YANG SUN: By you.

SHUI TA: What could you do about it?

YANG SUN: I could submit for discussion — my position in the firm.

SHUI TA: You are now my manager. In return for a more . . . appropriate position, you might agree to drop the inquiry into your ex-fiancée's whereabouts?

YANG SUN: I might.

SHUI TA: What position *would* be more appropriate?

YANG SUN: The one at the top.

SHUI TA: My own? *(Silence.)* And if I preferred to throw you out on your neck?

YANG SUN: I'd come back on my feet. With suitable escort.

SHUI TA: The police?

YANG SUN: The police.

SHUI TA: And when the police found no one?

YANG SUN: I might ask them not to overlook the back room. *(Ending the pretence)* In short, Mr. Shui Ta, my interest in this young woman has not been officially terminated. I should like to see more of her. *(Into* SHUI TA'S *face)* Besides, she's pregnant and needs a friend. *(He moves to the door.)* I shall talk about it with the water seller.

Exit. SHUI TA *is rigid for a moment, then he quickly goes into the back room. He returns with Shen Te's belongings: underwear, etc. He takes a long look at the shawl of the previous scene. He then wraps the things in a bundle, which, upon hearing a noise, he hides under the table. Enter* MRS. MI TZU *and* MR. SHU FU. *They put away their umbrellas and galoshes.*

MRS. MI TZU: I thought your manager was here, Mr. Shui Ta. He combines charm with business in a way that can only be to the advantage of all of us.

SHU FU: You sent for us, Mr. Shui Ta?

SHUI TA: The factory is in trouble.

SHU FU: It always is.

SHUI TA: The police are threatening to close us down unless I can show that the extension of our facilities is imminent.

SHU FU: Mr. Shui Ta, I'm sick and tired of your constantly expanding projects. I place cabins at your cousin's disposal; you make a factory of them. I hand your cousin a check; you present it. Your cousin disappears; you find the cabins too small and start talking of yet more—

SHUI TA: Mr. Shu Fu, I'm authorized to inform you that Miss Shen Te's return is now imminent.

SHU FU: Imminent? It's becoming his favorite word.

MRS. MI TZU: Yes, what does it mean?

SHUI TA: Mrs. Mi Tzu, I can pay you exactly half what you asked for your buildings. Are you ready to inform the police that I am taking them over?

MRS. MI TZU: Certainly, if I can take over your manager.

SHU FU: What?

MRS. MI TZU: He's so efficient.

SHUI TA: I'm afraid I need Mr. Yang Sun.

MRS. MI TZU: So do I.

SHUI TA: He will call on you tomorrow.

SHU FU: So much the better. With Shen Te likely to turn up at any moment, the presence of that young man is hardly in good taste.

SHUI TA: So we have reached a settlement. In what was once the good Shen Te's little shop we are laying the foundations for the great Mr. Shui Ta's twelve magnificent super tobacco markets. You will bear in mind that though they call me the Tobacco King of Setzuan, it is my cousin's interests that have been served...

VOICES (off): The police, the police! Going to the tobacco shop! Something must have happened!

Enter YANG SUN, WONG, *and the* POLICEMAN.

POLICEMAN: Quiet there, quiet, quiet! (*They quiet down.*) I'm sorry, Mr. Shui Ta, but there's a report that you've been depriving Miss Shen Te of her freedom. Not that I believe all I hear, but the whole city's in an uproar.

SHUI TA: That's a lie.

POLICEMAN: Mr. Yang Sun has testified that he heard someone sobbing in the back room.

SHU FU: Mrs. Mi Tzu and myself will testify that no one here has been sobbing.

MRS. MI TZU: We have been quietly smoking our cigars.

POLICEMAN: Mr. Shui Ta, I'm afraid I shall have to take a look at that room. (*He does so. The room is empty.*) No one there, of course, sir.

YANG SUN: But I heard sobbing. What's that?

He finds the clothes.

WONG: Those are Shen Te's things. (*To crowd*) Shen Te's clothes are here!

VOICES (off, in sequence): Shen Te's clothes!

They've been found under the table!
Body of murdered girl still missing!
Tobacco King suspected!

POLICEMAN: Mr. Shui Ta, unless you can tell us where the girl is, I'll have to ask you to come along.

SHUI TA: I do not know.

POLICEMAN: I can't say how sorry I am, Mr. Shui Ta. *(He shows him the door.)*

SHUI TA: Everything will be cleared up in no time. There are still judges in Setzuan.

YANG SUN: I heard sobbing!

Wong's den. For the last time, the GODS *appear to the water sell-er in his dream. They have changed and show signs of a long jour-ney, extreme fatigue, and plenty of mishaps. The* FIRST *no longer has a hat; the* THIRD *has lost a leg; all three are barefoot.*

WONG: Illustrious ones, at last you're here. Shen Te's been gone for months and today her cousin's been arrested. They think he murdered her to get the shop. But I had a dream and in this dream Shen Te said her cousin was keeping her prisoner. You must find her for us, illustrious ones!

FIRST GOD: We've found very few good people anywhere, and even they didn't keep it up. Shen Te is still the only one that stayed good.

SECOND GOD: If she *has* stayed good.

WONG: Certainly she has. But she's vanished.

FIRST GOD: That's the last straw. All is lost!

SECOND GOD: A little moderation, dear colleague!

FIRST GOD *(plaintively)*: What's the good of moderation now? If she can't be found, we'll have to resign! The world is a terrible place! Nothing but misery, vulgarity, and waste! Even the countryside isn't what it used to be. The trees are getting their heads chopped off by telephone wires, and there's such a noise from all the gunfire, and I can't stand those heavy clouds of smoke, and—

THIRD GOD: The place is absolutely unlivable! Good intentions bring people to the brink of the abyss, and good deeds push them over the edge. I'm afraid our book of rules is destined for the scrap heap—

SECOND GOD: It's people! They're a worthless lot!

THIRD GOD: The world is too cold!

SECOND GOD: It's people! They're too weak!

FIRST GOD: Dignity, dear colleagues, dignity! Never despair! As for this world, didn't we agree that we only have to find one human being who can stand the place? Well, we found her. True, we lost her again. We must find her again, that's all! And at once!

They disappear.

10

Courtroom. Groups: SHU FU *and* MRS. MI TZU; YANG SUN *and* MRS. YANG; WONG, *the* CARPENTER, *the* GRAND-FATHER, *the* NIECE, *the* OLD MAN, *the* OLD WOMAN; MRS. SHIN, *the* POLICEMAN; *the* UNEMPLOYED MAN, *the* SISTER-IN-LAW.

OLD MAN: So much power isn't good for one man.

UNEMPLOYED MAN: And he's going to open twelve super to-bacco markets!

WIFE: One of the judges is a friend of Mr. Shu Fu's.

SISTER-IN-LAW: Another one accepted a present from Mr. Shui Ta only last night. A great fat goose.

OLD WOMAN (*to* WONG): And Shen Te is nowhere to be found.

WONG: Only the gods will ever know the truth.

POLICEMAN: Order in the court! My lords the judges!

Enter the THREE GODS *in judges' robes. We overhear their conversation as they pass along the footlights to their bench.*

THIRD GOD: We'll never get away with it, our certificates were so badly forged.

SECOND GOD: My predecessor's "sudden indigestion" will certainly cause comment.

FIRST GOD: But he *had* just eaten a whole goose.

UNEMPLOYED MAN: Look at that! *New* judges.

WONG: New judges. And what good ones!

The THIRD GOD *hears this, and turns to smile at* WONG. *The* GODS *sit. The* FIRST GOD *beats on the bench with his gavel. The* POLICEMAN *brings in* SHUI TA *who walks with lordly steps. He is whistled at.*

POLICEMAN (*to* SHUI TA): Be prepared for a surprise. The judges have been changed.

SHUI TA *turns quickly round, looks at them, and staggers.*

NIECE: What's the matter now?

WIFE: The great Tobacco King nearly fainted.

HUSBAND: Yes, as soon as he saw the new judges.

WONG: Does *he* know who they are?

SHUI TA *picks himself up, and the proceedings open.*

FIRST GOD: Defendant Shui Ta, you are accused of doing away with your cousin Shen Te in order to take possession of her business. Do you plead guilty or not guilty?

SHUI TA: Not guilty, my lord.

FIRST GOD (*thumbing through the documents of the case*): The first witness is the policeman. I shall ask him to tell us something of the respective reputations of Miss Shen Te and Mr. Shui Ta.

POLICEMAN. Miss Shen Te was a young lady who aimed to please, my lord. She liked to live and let live, as the saying goes. Mr. Shui Ta, on the other hand, is a man of principle. Though the generosity of Miss Shen Te forced him at times to abandon half measures, unlike the girl he was always on the side of the law, my lord. One time, he even unmasked a gang of thieves to whom his too trustful cousin had given shelter. The evidence, in short, my lord, proves that Mr. Shui Ta was *incapable* of the crime of which he stands accused!

FIRST GOD: I see. And are there others who could testify along, shall we say, the same lines?

SHU FU *rises.*

POLICEMAN (*whispering to* GODS): Mr. Shu Fu — a very important person.

FIRST GOD (*inviting him to speak*): Mr. Shu Fu!

SHU FU: Mr. Shui Ta is a businessman, my lord. Need I say more?

FIRST GOD: Yes.

SHU FU: Very well, I will. He is Vice President of the Council of Commerce and is about to be elected a Justice of the Peace. (*He returns to his seat.* MRS. MI TZU *rises.*)

WONG: Elected! *He* gave him the job!

With a gesture the FIRST GOD *asks who* MRS. MI TZU *is.*

POLICEMAN: Another very important person. Mrs. Mi Tzu.

FIRST GOD (*inviting her to speak*): Mrs. Mi Tzu!

MRS. MI TZU: My lord, as Chairman of the Committee on Social Work, I wish to call attention to just a couple of eloquent facts: Mr. Shui Ta not only has erected a model factory with model housing in our city, he is a regular contributor to our home for the disabled. (*She returns to her seat.*)

POLICEMAN (*whispering*): And she's a great friend of the judge that ate the goose!

FIRST GOD (*to the* POLICEMAN): Oh, thank you. What next? (*To the Court, genially*) Oh, yes. We should find out if any of the evidence is less favorable to the defendant.

WONG, *the* CARPENTER, *the* OLD MAN, *the* OLD WOMAN, *the* UNEMPLOYED MAN, *the* SISTER-IN-LAW, *and the* NIECE *come forward.*

POLICEMAN (*whispering*): Just the riffraff, my lord.

FIRST GOD (*addressing the "riffraff"*): Well, um, riffraff — do you know anything of the defendant, Mr. Shui Ta?

WONG: Too much, my lord.

UNEMPLOYED MAN: What don't we know, my lord.

CARPENTER: He ruined us.

SISTER-IN-LAW: He's a cheat.

NIECE: Liar.

WIFE: Thief.

BOY: Blackmailer.

BROTHER: Murderer.

FIRST GOD: Thank you. We should now let the defendant state his point of view.

SHUI TA: I only came on the scene when Shen Te was in danger of losing what I had understood was a gift from the gods. Because I did the filthy jobs which someone had to do, they hate me. My activities were restricted to the minimum, my lord.

SISTER-IN-LAW: He had us arrested!

SHUI TA: Certainly. You stole from the bakery!

SISTER-IN-LAW: Such concern for the bakery! You didn't want the shop for yourself, I suppose!

SHUI TA: I didn't want the shop overrun with parasites.

SISTER-IN-LAW: We had nowhere else to go.

SHUI TA: There were too many of you.

WONG: What about this old couple: Were *they* parasites?

OLD MAN: We lost our shop because of you!

OLD WOMAN: And we gave your cousin money!

SHUI TA: My cousin's fiancé was a flyer. The money had to go to *him*.

WONG: Did you care whether he flew or not? Did you care whether she married him or not? You wanted her to marry someone else!

(He points at SHU FU.)

SHUI TA: The flyer unexpectedly turned out to be a scoundrel.

YANG SUN *(jumping up)*: Which was the reason you made him your manager?

SHUI TA: Later on he improved.

WONG: And when he improved, you sold him to her?

(He points out MRS. MI TZU.)

SHUI TA: She wouldn't let me have her premises unless she had him to stroke her knees!

MRS. MI TZU: What? The man's a pathological liar. *(To him)* Don't mention my property to me as long as you live! Murderer! *(She rustles off, in high dudgeon.)*

YANG SUN *(pushing in)*: My lord, I wish to speak for the defendant.

SISTER-IN-LAW: Naturally. He's your employer.

UNEMPLOYED MAN: And the worst slave driver in the country.

MRS. YANG: That's a lie! My lord, Mr. Shui Ta is a great man. He...

YANG SUN: He's this and he's that, but he is not a murderer, my lord. Just fifteen minutes before his arrest I heard Shen Te's voice in his own back room.

FIRST GOD: Oh? Tell us more!

YANG SUN: I heard sobbing, my lord!

FIRST GOD: But lots of women sob, we've been finding.

YANG SUN: Could I fail to recognize her voice?

SHU FU: No, you made her sob so often yourself, young man!

YANG SUN: Yes. But I also made her happy. Till he *(pointing at* SHUI TA) decided to sell her to you!

SHUI TA: Because you didn't love her.

WONG: Oh, no: it was for the money, my lord!

SHUI TA: And what was the money for, my lord? For the poor! And for Shen Te so she could go on being good!

WONG: For the poor? That he sent to his sweatshops? And why didn't you let Shen Te be good when you signed the big check?

SHUI TA: For the child's sake, my lord.

CARPENTER: What about *my* children? What did he do about them?

SHUI TA *is silent.*

WONG: The shop was to be a fountain of goodness. That was the gods' idea. You came and spoiled it!

SHUI TA: If I hadn't, it would have run dry!

MRS. SHIN: There's a lot in that, my lord.

WONG: What have you done with the good Shen Te, bad man?
She *was* good, my lords, she was, I swear it!
(He raises his hand in an oath.)

THIRD GOD: What's happened to your hand, water seller?

WONG *(pointing to SHUI TA)*: It's all his fault, my lord, *she*
was going to send me to a doctor — *(To SHUI TA)* You were
her worst enemy!

SHUI TA: I was her only friend!

WONG: Where is she then? Tell us where your good friend is!
*The excitement of this exchange has run through the whole
crowd.*

ALL: Yes, where is she? Where is Shen Te? *(Etc.)*

SHUI TA: Shen Te . . . had to go.

WONG: Where? Where to?

SHUI TA: I cannot tell you! I cannot tell you!

ALL: Why? Why did she have to go away? *(Etc.)*

WONG *(into the din with the first words, but talking on beyond
the others)*: Why not, why not? Why did she have to go away?

SHUI TA *(shouting)*: Because you'd all have torn her to shreds,
that's why! My lords, I have a request. Clear the court! When
only the judges remain, I will make a confession.

ALL *(except WONG, who is silent, struck by the new turn of events)*:
So he's guilty? He's confessing! *(Etc.)*

FIRST GOD *(using the gavel)*: Clear the court!

POLICEMAN: Clear the court!

WONG: Mr. Shui Ta has met his match this time.

MRS. SHIN *(with a gesture toward the judges)*: You're in for a
little surprise.

The court is cleared. Silence.

SHUI TA: Illustrious ones!

The GODS look at each other, not quite believing their ears.

SHUI TA: Yes, I recognize you!

SECOND GOD *(taking matters in hand, sternly)*: What have you
done with our good woman of Setzuan?

SHUI TA: I have a terrible confession to make: I am she!
   (*He takes off his mask, and tears away his clothes.* SHEN TE
   stands there.)
SECOND GOD: Shen Te!
SHEN TE: Shen Te, yes. Shui Ta *and* Shen Te. Both.
   Your injunction
   To be good and yet to live
   Was a thunderbolt:
   It has torn me in two
   I can't tell how it was
   But to be good to others
   And myself at the same time
   I could not do it
   Your world is not an easy one, illustrious ones!
   When we extend our hand to a beggar, he tears it off for
      us
   When we help the lost, we are lost ourselves
   And so
   Since not to eat is to die
   Who can long refuse to be bad?
   As I lay prostrate beneath the weight of good intentions
   Ruin stared me in the face
   It was when I was unjust that I ate good meat
   And hobnobbed with the mighty
   Why?
   Why are bad deeds rewarded?
   Good ones punished?
   I enjoyed giving
   I truly wished to be the Angel of the Slums
   But washed by a foster-mother in the water of the gutter
   I developed a sharp eye
   The time came when pity was a thorn in my side
   And, later, when kind words turned to ashes in my mouth
   And anger took over

I became a wolf
Find me guilty, then, illustrious ones,
But know:
All that I have done I did
To help my neighbor
To love my lover
And to keep my little one from want
For your great, godly deeds, I was too poor, too small.
Pause.

FIRST GOD *(shocked)*: Don't go on making yourself miserable, Shen Te! We're overjoyed to have found you!

SHEN TE: I'm telling you I'm the bad man who committed all those crimes!

FIRST GOD *(using — or failing to use — his ear trumpet)*: The good woman who did all those good deeds?

SHEN TE: Yes, but the bad man too!

FIRST GOD *(as if something had dawned)*: Unfortunate coincidences! Heartless neighbors!

THIRD GOD *(shouting in his ear)*: But how is she to continue?

FIRST GOD: Continue? Well, she's a strong, healthy girl . . .

SECOND GOD: You didn't hear what she said!

FIRST GOD: I heard every word! She is confused, that's all! *(He begins to bluster)* And what about this book of rules — we can't renounce our rules, can we? *(More quietly)* Should the world be changed? How? By whom? The world should not be changed! *(At a sign from him, the lights turn pink, and music plays.)*[1]

And now the hour of parting is at hand.
Dost thou behold, Shen Te, yon fleecy cloud?

---

1. The rest of this scene has been adapted for the many American theatres that do not have "fly-space" to lower things from on ropes. The translation in the first Minnesota edition, following the German exactly, is reprinted here in the bracketed passage on pages 105–6. E.B.

It is our chariot. At a sign from me
'Twill come and take us back from whence we came
Above the azure vault and silver stars. . . .

SHEN TE: No! Don't go, illustrious ones!

FIRST GOD:

Our cloud has landed now in yonder field
From which it will transport us back to heaven.
Farewell, Shen Te, let not thy courage fail thee. . . .

Exeunt GODS.

SHEN TE: What about the old couple? They've lost their shop!
What about the water seller and his hand? And I've got to
defend myself against the barber, because I don't love him!
And against Sun, because I do love him! How? How?

SHEN TE'S *eyes follow the* GODS *as they are imagined to step
into a cloud which rises and moves forward over the orchestra
and up beyond the balcony.*

FIRST GOD *(from on high)*: We have faith in you, Shen Te!

SHEN TE: There'll be a child. And he'll have to be fed. I can't
stay here. Where shall I go?

FIRST GOD: Continue to be good, good woman of Setzuan!

SHEN TE: I need my bad cousin!

FIRST GOD: But not very often!

SHEN TE: Once a week at least!

FIRST GOD: Once a month will be quite enough!

SHEN TE *(shrieking)*: No, no! Help!

But the cloud continues to recede as the GODS *sing.*

VALEDICTORY HYMN

What rapture, oh, it is to know
A good thing when you see it
And having seen a good thing, oh,
What rapture 'tis to flee it

Be good, sweet maid of Setzuan
Let Shui Ta be clever

Departing, we forget the man
Remember your endeavor

Because through all the length of days
Her goodness faileth never
Sing hallelujah! Make Shen Te's
Good name live on forever!

SHEN TE: Help!

[FIRST GOD:

And now... *(He makes a sign and music is heard. Rosy
light.)* let us return.
This little world has much engaged us.
Its joy and its sorrow have refreshed and pained us.
Up there, however, beyond the stars,
We shall gladly think of you, Shen Te, the good woman
Who bears witness to our spirit down below,
Who, in cold darkness, carries a little lamp!
Good-bye! Do it well!

*He makes a sign and the ceiling opens. A pink cloud comes down.
On it the* THREE GODS *rise, very slowly.*

SHEN TE: Oh, don't, illustrious ones! Don't go away! Don't
leave me! How can I face the good old couple who've lost
their store and the water seller with his stiff hand? And how
can I defend myself from the barber whom I do not love
and from Sun whom I do love? And I am with child. Soon
there'll be a little son who'll want to eat. I can't stay here!
*(She turns with a hunted look toward the door which will let
her tormentors in.)*

FIRST GOD: You can do it. Just be good and everything will
turn out well!

*Enter the witnesses. They look with surprise at the judges float-
ing on their pink cloud.*

WONG: Show respect! The gods have appeared among us! Three
of the highest gods have come to Setzuan to find a good human being. They had found one already, but...

FIRST GOD: No "but"! Here she is!

ALL: Shen Te!

FIRST GOD: She has not perished. She was only hidden. She will stay with you. A good human being!

SHEN TE: But I need my cousin!

FIRST GOD: Not too often!

SHEN TE: At least once a week!

FIRST GOD: Once a month. That's enough!

SHEN TE: Oh, don't go away, illustrious ones! I haven't told you everything! I need you desperately!

The GODS *sing.*

THE TRIO OF THE VANISHING GODS OF THE CLOUD

> Unhappily we cannot stay
> More than a fleeting year.
> If we watch our find too long
> It will disappear.
>
> Here the golden light of truth
> With shadow is alloyed
> Therefore now we ask your leave
> To go back to our void.

SHEN TE: Help!

Her cries continue through the song.

> Since our search is over now
> Let us fast ascend!
> The good woman of Setzuan
> Praise we at the end!

As SHEN TE *stretches out her arms to them in desperation, they disappear above, smiling and waving.*]

Epilogue

You're thinking, aren't you, that this is no right
Conclusion to the play you've seen tonight?
After a tale, exotic, fabulous,
A nasty ending was slipped up on us.
We feel deflated too. We too are nettled
To see the curtain down and nothing settled.
How could a better ending be arranged?
Could one change people? Can the world be changed?
Would new gods do the trick? Will atheism?
Moral rearmament? Materialism?
It is for you to find a way, my friends,
To help good men arrive at happy ends.
You write the happy ending to the play!
There must, there must, there's got to be a way![2]

---

2. When I first received the German manuscript of *Good Woman* from Brecht in 1945 it had no Epilogue. He wrote it a little later, influenced by misunderstandings of the ending in the press on the occasion of the Viennese première of the play. I believe that the Epilogue has sometimes been spoken by the actress playing Shen Te, but the actor playing Wong might be a shrewder choice, since the audience has already accepted him as a kind of chorus. On the other hand, it is not Wong who should deliver the Epilogue: whichever actor delivers it should drop the characters he has been playing. E.B.

Selected Bibliography

PLAYS BY BERTOLT BRECHT

Baal, 1918

Trommeln in der Nacht (Drums in the Night), 1918–20

Im Dickicht der Städte (In the Jungle of the Cities), 1921–23

Mann ist Mann (A Man's a Man), 1924–25

Die Dreigroschenoper (The Threepenny Opera), 1928

Aufstieg und Fall der Stadt Mahagonny (Rise and Fall of the City of Mahagonny), 1928–29

Das Badener Lehrstück vom Einverständnis (The Didactic Play of Baden: On Consent), 1928–29

Die heilige Johanna der Schlachthöfe (St. Joan of the Stockyards), 1929–30

Die Massnahme (The Measures Taken), 1930

Die Mutter (The Mother), 1930–32

Die Rundköpfe und die Spitzköpfe (Roundheads and Peakheads) 1931–36

Furcht und Elend des Dritten Reiches (Fear and Misery in the Third Reich), 1935–38

Mutter Courage und ihre Kinder (Mother Courage and Her Children), 1939

Das Verhör des Lukullus (The Trial of Lucullus), 1939
Leben des Galilei (Galileo), 1938–40
Der gute Mensch von Sezuan (The Good Woman of Setzuan),
    1938–40
Herr Puntila und sein knecht Matti (Mr. Puntila and His Man,
    Matti), 1940–41
Der aufhaltsame Aufstieg des Arturo Ui (The Resistible Rise of
    Arturo Ui), 1941
Schweyk im zweiten Weltkrieg (Schweik in the Second World War),
    1941–44
Die Gesichte der Simone Machard (The Visions of Simone
    Machard), 1941–44
Der kaukakische Kreidekreis (The Caucasian Chalk Circle), 1944–45
Antigone, 1947
Die Tage der Kommune (Days of the Commune), 1948–49
Der Hofmeister (The Tutor), 1950
Turandot, 1953–54, unfinished

TRANSLATED POEMS AND SONGS

Selected Poems. Translated by H.R. Hays. New York: Reynal and
    Hitchcock, 1947.
Manual of Piety. Translated by Eric Bentley. New York: Grove Press,
    1966.
The Brecht-Eisler Song Book. Edited, with translations by Eric
    Bentley. New York: Oak Publications, 1967 (later taken over by
    Music Sales Corporation, New York).
Poems 1913–1956. Edited by John Willett and Ralph Mannheim.
    London and New York: Methuen, 1976.

THE BRECHT-BENTLEY RECORDINGS

Bentley on Brecht: A Bertolt Brecht Miscellany. Performed by Eric
    Bentley. Folkways, FH 5434.
Brecht Before the Un-American Activities Committee. A recording of
    the hearing. Folkways, FD 5531.

The Elephant Calf. The National Company cast album. Folkways, FL 9831.

The Exception and the Rule. The Off-Broadway cast album with Joseph Chaikin. Folkways, FL 9849.

A Man's a Man. The Off-Broadway cast album. Music by Joe Raposo. Spoken Arts, SA 870.

Songs of Hanns Eisler. Most of them to words by Brecht. Folkways, FH 5433.

The five Folkways recordings were originally twelve-inch LPs but today are distributed by Smithsonian Folkways as cassette tapes and CDs. The Spoken Arts album is available from P.O. Box 100, New Rochelle, NY 10802-0100.

BIOGRAPHY AND CRITICISM

Bentley, Eric. *The Playwright as Thinker.* New York: Reynal and Hitchcock, 1946.

———. *The Brecht Commentaries.* New York: Grove Press; London: Eyre Methuen, 1981.

———. *The Brecht Memoir.* New York: PAJ Publications, 1985.

———. *Bertolt Brecht: A Study Guide.* New York: Grove, 1995.

———. *Bentley on Brecht.* New York: Applause, 1998.

Demetz, Peter, ed. *Brecht: A Collection of Critical Essays.* Englewood Cliffs, N.J.: Prentice-Hall, 1962.

Esslin, Martin. *Brecht: The Man and His Work.* Garden City, N.Y.: Doubleday Anchor, 1960.

Fuegi, John. *Bertolt Brecht: Chaos according to Plan.* Cambridge: Cambridge University Press, 1987.

———. *Brecht and Company.* New York: Grove, 1994.

Hayman, Ronald. *Brecht: a Biography.* New York: Oxford University Press, 1983.

Lyon, James K. *Bertolt Brecht in America.* Princeton: Princeton University Press, 1980.

Munk, Erika, ed. *Brecht.* New York: Bantam Books, 1972.

Spalter, Max. *Brecht's Tradition.* Baltimore, Md.: Johns Hopkins Press, 1967.

Völker, Klaus. *Brecht Chronicle.* Trans. Fred Wieck. New York: The Seabury Press, 1975.

————. *Brecht: A Biography.* Trans. John Nowell. New York: The Seabury Press, 1978.

Willett, John. *The Theatre of Bertolt Brecht.* Norfolk, Conn.: New Directions, 1959.

Witt, Hubert, ed. *Brecht as They Knew Him.* Trans. John Peet. New York: International Publishers, 1974.

Bertolt Brecht was born in Germany in 1898 and grew up amid the violence and turbulence of twentieth-century Europe. His experiences as a medical orderly in World War I and as a witness to the political and social turmoil in defeated Germany helped shape the Marxist vision that informed his poems and plays, beginning with *Baal* in 1918. One of the most influential writers in Germany in the years before 1933, with such triumphs to his credit as *The Threepenny Opera* and *Rise and Fall of the City of Mahagonny* (both with music by Kurt Weill), Brecht fled the country upon the Nazi assumption of power. *The Good Woman of Setzuan* was written in 1939–40, during a period of exile spent in Finland, and *The Caucasian Chalk Circle* was written in Hollywood in 1944. After World War II, Brecht returned to Europe, living first in Switzerland and then in East Germany, where he died in 1956.

Eric Bentley, one of the foremost authorities on the modern theater and a longtime intimate of Bertolt Brecht, has translated and edited most of Brecht's major works. He was born in Bolton, Lancashire, in 1916 and became an American citizen in 1948. He began his professional career as a scholar, went on to become a drama critic and translator, and then became a playwright. He was inducted into the Theatre Hall of Fame in 1998.